PEACE AND BREAD IN TIME OF WAR

PEACE AND BREAD IN TIME OF WAR

Jane Addams

www.General-Books.net

Publication Data:

Title: Peace and Bread in Time of War
Author: Jane Addams
Reprinted: 2010, General Books, Memphis, Tennessee, USA
Publisher: The Macmillan Company
Publication date: 1922
Subjects: World War, 1914-1918
History / Military / General
History / Military / World War I
Political Science / Public Policy / Social Services Welfare
Political Science / Peace
BISAC subject codes: HIS027000, HIS027090, POL019000, POL034000

1

PEACE AND BREAD IN TIME OF WAR

FOREWORD

The following pages are the outgrowth of an attempt to write a brief history of the efforts for peace made by a small group of women in the United States during the European War, and of their connection with the women of other countries, as together they became organized into the Womens International League for Peace and Freedom.

Such a history would of course be meaningless, unless it portrayed the scruples and convictions upon which these efforts were based. During the writing of it, however, I found myself so increasingly reluctant to interpret the motives of other people that at length I confined all analysis of motives to my own. As my reactions were in no wise unusual, I can only hope that the autobiographical portrayal of them may prove to be fairly typical and interpretative of many like-minded people who, as the great war progressed, gradually found themselves the protagonists of that most unpopular of all causes–peace in time of war.

I was occasionally reminded of a dictum found on the cover of a long since extinct magazine entitled "The Arena," which read somewhat in this wise: "We do not possess our ideas, they possess us, and force us into the arena to fight for them." It would be more fitting for our group to say "to be martyred for them," but candor compels the confession that no such dignified fate was permitted us. Our portion was the odium accorded those who, because they are not allowed to state their own cause, suffer constantly from inimical misrepresentation and are often placed in the position of seeming to defend what is a mere travesty of their convictions.

We realize, therefore, that even the kindest of readers must perforce still look at our group through the distorting spectacles he was made to wear during the long period of war propaganda.

As the writing progressed I entitled the book "Peace and Bread in Time of War." Not because the first two words were the touching slogan of war-weary Russian peasants, but because peace and bread had become inseparably connected in my mind.

I shall consider myself fortunate if I am able to convey to the reader the inevitability of the relationship.

Hull-House,
Chicago.

PEACE AND BREAD IN TIME OF WAR
CHAPTER I.
AT THE BEGINNING OF THE GREAT WAR.

When the news came to America of the opening hostilities which were the beginning of the European Conflict, the reaction against war, as such, was almost instantaneous throughout the country. This was most strikingly registered in the newspaper cartoons and comments which expressed astonishment that such an archaic institution should be revived in modern Europe. A procession of women led by the daughter of William Lloyd Garrison walked the streets of New York City in protest against war and the sentiment thus expressed, if not the march itself, was universally approved by the press.

Certain professors, with the full approval of their universities, set forth with clarity and sometimes with poignancy the conviction that a war would inevitably interrupt all orderly social ad vance and at its end the long march of civilization would have to be taken up again much nearer to the crude beginnings of human progress.

The Carnegie Endowment sent several people lecturing through the country upon the history of the Peace movement and the various instrumentalities designed to be used in a war crisis such as this. I lectured in twelve of the leading colleges, where I found the audiences of young people both large and eager. The questions which they put were often penetrating, sometimes touching or wistful, but almost never bellicose or antagonistic. Doubtless there were many students of the more belligerent type who did not attend the lectures and occasionally a professor, invariably one of the older men, rose in the audience to uphold the traditional glories of warfare. I also recall a tea under the shadow of Columbia which was divided into two spirited camps, but I think on the whole it is fair to say that in the fall of 1914 the young people in a dozen of the leading colleges of the East were eager for knowledge as to all the international devices which had been established for substituting rational negotiation for war. There seemed to have been a somewhat general reading of Brailsfords "War of Steel and Gold" and of Norman Angells "Great Illusion."

It was in the early fall of 1914 that a small group of social workers held the first of a series of meetings at the Henry Street Settlement in New York, trying to formulate the reaction to war on the part of those who for many years had devoted their energies to the reduction of devastating poverty. We believed that the endeavor to nurture human life even in its most humble and least promising forms had crossed national boundaries; that those who had given years to its service had become convinced that nothing of social value can be obtained save through wide-spread public opinion and the cooperation of all civilized nations. Many members of this group meeting in the Henry Street Settlement had lived in the cosmopolitan districts of American cities. All of us, through long experience among the immigrants from many nations, were convinced that a friendly and cooperative relationship was constantly becoming more possible between all peoples. We believed that war, seeking its end through coercion, not only interrupted but fatally reversed this process of cooperating good will which, if it had a chance, would eventually include the human family itself.

The European War was already dividing our immigrant neighbors from each other. We could not imagine asking ourselves whether the parents of a child who needed help were Italians, and therefore on the side of the Allies, or Dalmatians, and therefore on the side of the Central Powers. Such a question was as remote as if during the Balkan war we had anxiously inquired whether the parents were Macedonians or Montenegrins although at one time that distinction had been of paramount importance to many of our neighbors. We revolted not only against the cruelty and barbarity of war, but even more against the reversal of human relationships which war implied. We protested against the "curbed intelligence" and the "thwarted good will," when both a free mind and unfettered kindliness are so sadly needed in human affairs. In the light of the charge made later that pacifists were indifferent to the claims of justice it is interesting to recall that we thus early emphasized the fact that a sense of justice had become the keynote to the best political and social activity in this generaton, but we also believed that justice between men or between nations can be achieved only through understanding and fellowship, and that a finely tempered sense of justice, which alone is of any service in modern civilization, cannot possibly be secured in the storm and stress of war. This is not only because war inevitably arouses the more primitive antagonisms, but because the spirit of fighting burns away all those impulses, certainly towards the enemy, which foster the will to justice. We were therefore certain that if war prevailed, all social efforts would be cast into an earlier and coarser mold.

The results of these various discussions were finally put together by Mr. Paul Kellogg, editor of The Survey, and the statement entitled "Toward the Peace that Shall Last" was given a wide circulation. Reading it now, it appears to be somewhat exaggerated in tone because we have perforce grown accustomed to a world of widespread war with its inevitable consequences of divisions and animosities.

The heartening effects of these meetings were long felt by many of the social workers as they proceeded in their different ways to do what they could against the rising tide of praise for the use of war technique in the worlds affairs. One type of person present at this original conference felt that he must make his protest against war even at the risk of going to jail–in fact two of the men did so testify and took the consequences; another type performed all non-combatant service open to them through the Red Cross and other agencies throughout the years of the war although privately holding to their convictions as best they might; a third, although condemning war in the abstract were convinced of the righteousness of this particular war and that it would end all wars; still others felt, after war was declared in the United States, that they must surrender all private judgment, and abide by the decision of the majority.

I venture to believe, however, that none of the social workers present at that gathering who had been long identified with the poor and the disinherited, actually accepted participation in the war without a great struggle, if only because of the reversal in the whole theory and practice of their daily living.

Several organizations were formed during the next few months, with which we became identified; Miss Wald was the first president of the Union Against Militarism, and I became chairman of what was called the Womens Peace Party. The impulse for the latter organization came from Europe when, in the early winter of 1914, the great war was discussed from the public platform in the United States by two women, well known suffragists and publicists, who nationally represented opposing sides of the conflict. Mrs. Peth-ick Lawrence of England first brought to American audiences a series of "War Aims" as defined by the "League of Democratic Control" in London, and Mde. Rosika Schwimmer, coming from Budapest, hoped to arouse American women to join their European sisters in a general protest against war. Occasionally they spoke from the same platform in a stirring indictment of "the common enemy of mankind." They were unwilling to leave the United States until they had organized at least a small group pledged to the ad vocacy of both objects; the discussion of reasonable terms of peace, and a protest against war as a method of settling international difficulties.

The Womens Peace Party itself was the outcome of a two days convention held in Washington concluding a series of meetings in different cities addressed by Mrs. Lawrence and Madame Schwimmer. The "call" to the convention was issued by Mrs. Carrie Chapman Catt and myself, and on January 10, 1915, the new organization was launched at a mass meeting of 3000 people. A ringing preamble written by Mrs. Anna Garlin Spencer was adopted with the following platform: 1. The immediate calling of a convention of neutral nations in the interest of early peace.

2. Limitation of armaments and the nationalization of their manufacture.

3. Organized opposition to militarism in our own country.

4. Education of youth in the ideals of peace.

5. Democratic control of foreign policies.

6. The further humanizing of governments by the extension of the suffrage to women.

7. "Concert of Nations" to supersede "Balance of Power."

8. Action towards the gradual re-organization of the world to substitute Law for War.

9. The substitution of economic pressure and of non-intercourse for rival armies and navies.

10. Removal of the economic causes of war.

n. The appointment by our government of a commission of men and women with an adequate appropriation to promote international peace.

Of course all the world has since become familiar with these "Points," but at the time of their adoption as a platform they were newer and somewhat startling.

The first one, as a plan for "continuous mediation," had been presented to the convention by Miss Julia G. Wales of the University of Wisconsin, who had already placed it before the legislature of the State. Both houses had given it their approval, and had sent it on with recommendations for adoption to the Congress of the United States. The plan was founded upon the assumption that the question of peace was a question of terms; that every country desired peace at the earliest possible moment, that peace could be had on terms satisfactory to itself. The plan suggested an International Commission of Experts to sit as long as the war continued, with scientific but no diplomatic function; such a commission should explore the issues involved in the struggle in order to make proposals to the belligerents in a spirit of constructive internationalism. Miss Wales not only defined such a Commission, but presented a most convincing argument in its behalf, and we deliberately made the immediate calling of a Conference of Neutrals the first plank in our new platform.

The officers of the newly formed society were: Mrs. Anna Garlin Spencer and Mrs. Henry Vil-lard of New York, Mrs. Lucia Ames Mead and Mrs. Glendower Evans of Boston, Mrs. Louis F. Post and Mrs. John J. White of Washington. From Chicago, where headquarters were established, were Mrs. Harriet Thomas as executive officer, Miss Breckenridge of the University of Chicago as treasurer, and myself as Chairman.

All of the officers had long been identified with existing Peace organizations, but felt the need of something more active than the older societies promised to afford. The first plank of our platform, the Conference of Neutrals, seemed so important and withal so reasonable, that our officers in the month following the founding of the organization, with Louis Lochner, secretary of the Chicago Peace Society, issued a call to every public organization in the United States whose constitution, so far as we could discover, contained a plank setting forth the obligations of internationalism. These organizations of course included hundreds of mutual benefit societies, of trade unions and socialist groups, as well as the more formal peace and reform bodies. The call invited them to attend a National Emergency Peace Conference at Chicago in March, and to join a Federation of Peace Forces. A very interesting group responded to the invitation, and the Conference, resulting in the formation of the proposed Federation, also held large mass meetings urging the call of a Conference of Neutrals.

The Womens Peace Party, during the first few months of its existence, grew rapidly, with flourishing branches in California and in Minnesota, as well as in the eastern states. The Boston branch eventually opened headquarters on the first floor of a building in the busy part of Boylston Street, and with a membership of twenty-five hundred, carried on a vigorous campaign among the doubting, making public opinion both for reasonable peace terms and for a possible shortening of the war. A number of the leading organizations of women became affiliated branches of the Womens Peace Party. Women everywhere seemed eager for literature and lectures, and as the movement antedated by six months the organization of the League to Enforce Peace, we had the field all to ourselves.

In the early months of 1915, it was still comparatively easy to get people together in the name of Peace, and the members of the new organization scarcely realized that they were placing themselves on the side of an unpopular cause. One obvious task was to unite with other organizations in setting out a constructive program with which an international public should become so familiar that an effective demand for its fulfillment could be made at the end of the war. This latter undertaking had been brilliantly inaugurated by The League of Democratic Control in England, and two months after our Washington Convention, "The Central Organization for a Durable Peace" was founded in Holland. The American branch of the "Association for the Promotion of International Friendship Among the Churches" also was active and maintained its own representative in Europe. As a neutral, he at that time was able to go from one country to another, and to meet in Holland with Churchmen from both sides of the conflict. We always found him most willing to cooperate with our plans at home and abroad. His successor, George Nasmyth, was also a sturdy friend of ours, and we keenly felt the tragedy of his death at Geneva, in 1920.

Through the very early spring of 1915, out of our eagerness, we tried all sorts of new methods of propaganda, new at least so far as peace societies were concerned. A poem which had appeared in the London Nation portraying the bewilderment of humble Belgians and Germans sent suddenly to arms, was set to Beethovens music and, through the efforts of the Womens Peace Party, sung in many towns and cities in the United States by the Fuller sisters, three young English women, whose voices were most appealing. The Carnegie Endowment for International Peace gave us a grant of five thousand dollars with which we financed the Little Theatre Company of Chicago, in the production of Gilbert Murrays version of the Trojan women by Euripides. The play was given throughout the country, including the Panama Exposition at San Francisco. The beautiful lines were beautifully rendered. An audience invariably fell into a solemn mood as the age-old plaint of war-weary women cheated even of death, issued from the darkened stage, reciting not the glory of War, but "shame and blindness and a world swallowed up in night."

In March, 1915, we received an invitation signed by Dutch, British and Belgian women to an International Congress of Women to be held at The Hague, April 28 to May 1, at which I was asked to preside. The Congress was designed as a protest against war, in which it was hoped women from all nations would join. I had previously met several of the signers at the International Suffrage Conference and elsewhere. I knew them to be women of great courage and ability, and I had long warmly admired Dr. Al-letta Jacobs of Amsterdam, whose name led the list.

A delegation of forty-seven women from the
United States accepted the invitation, most of them members of the new Womens Peace Party. All of the delegates were obliged to pay their own expenses, and to trust somewhat confidingly to the usefulness of the venture. We set sail for Holland in the middle of April, on the Dutch ship Noordam, in which we were almost the only passengers. We were thus able to use the salon for daily conferences and lectures on the history of the Peace Movement. As the ship, steadied by a loose cargo of wheat, calmly proceeded on her way, our spirits rose, and all went well until, within four days of the date set for the opening of the Conference, the Noordam came to a standstill in the English Channel directly off the cliffs of Dover, where we faintly heard booming of cannon, and saw air and marine craft of every conceivable make and kind. The first English newspapers which came on board informed us of the sharp opposition to the holding of our Congress, lest it weaken the morale of the soldiers. We were called "Peacettes" and the enterprise loaded with ridicule of the sort with which we later became only too familiar. During the three days the ship hung at anchor there

was much telegraphing to all the people of political influence whom any one of us knew in England and several cables were sent to Washington.

Whether due to these or not, the Noordam finally received permission to proceed on her way and we landed in Rotterdam two hours before the opening of the Congress. We from the United States were more fortunate than the English delegation. The North Sea had been declared closed to all traffic the very day they were to start, and eighty-seven of them waited at a port during the entire session of The Hague Congress, first for boats and later for flying machines, neither of which ever came. Fortunately three Englishwomen had arrived earlier, and made a small but most able delegation from Great Britain.

The delegates at the Congress represented twelve different countries; they were all suffragists and believers in the settlement of international disputes by pacific means. Belligerent as well as neutral nations were represented, with sometimes two thousand visitors in attendance, all of whom had paid an entrance fee but were not allowed to participate in the deliberations. The sessions were characterized by efficiency and scrupulous courtesy, not without a touch of dignity, as became the solemn theme. All discussion of the causes of the war and of its conduct was prohibited, but discussions on the terms of peace and the possible prevention of future wars, were carried on with much intelligence and fervor.

Gradually the police, who filled the galleries at the first meetings, were withdrawn as it became evident that there was to be no disturbance or untoward excitement. A moment of great interest was the entrance of the two Belgian delegates, who shook hands with the German delegation before they took their places beside them on the platform, dedicated to "a passionate human sympathy, not inconsistent with patriotism, but transcending it." All the women from the belligerent countries in leaving home to attend the Congress had dared ridicule and every sort of difficulty; they had also met the supreme test of a womans conscience—of differing with those whom she loves in the hour of their deepest affliction. For men in the heat of war were at the best sceptical of the value of the Congress and many of them were actually hostile to it; in fact the delegates from one of the northern German cities were put in jail when they returned home, solely on thq charge of having attended a Congress in which women from the enemy countries were sitting.

A series of resolutions was very carefully drawn as a result of the three days deliberations. A committee, consisting of two women from each country, called "The Womens International Committee for Permanent Peace," was organized and established headquarters at Amsterdam.

At its last session, the Congress voted that its resolutions, especially the one on a Conference of Neutrals, should be carried by a delegation of women from the neutral countries to the Premier and Minister of Foreign Affairs of each of the belligerent countries, and by a delegation of women from the belligerent countries to the same officials in the neutral nations. As a result fourteen countries were visited in May and June, 1915, by delegates from the Congress.

As women, it was possible for us, from belligerent and neutral nations alike, to carry forward an interchange of question and answer between capitals which were barred to each other. Everywhere, save from one official in France, we heard the same opinion expressed by these men of the governments responsible for the promotion of the war; each one said that his country would be ready to stop the war immediately if some honorable method of securing peace were provided; each one disclaimed responsibility for the continuance of the war; each one predicted European bankruptcy if the war were prolonged, and each one grew pale and distressed as he spoke of the loss of his gallant young countrymen; two of them with ill-concealed emotion referred to the loss of their own sons.

We heard much the same words spoken in Downing Street as those spoken in Wilhelm-strasse, in Vienna as-in Petrograd, in Budapest as in Havre, where the Belgians had their temporary government. "My country would not find anything unfriendly in such action by the neu trals," was the assurance given us by the Foreign minister of one of the great belligerents. "My Government would place no obstacle in the way of its institution," said the Minister of an opposing nation. "What are the neutrals waiting for?" said a third.

Our confidence as to the feasibility of the plan for a Conference of Neutrals also increased. "You are right," said one Minister, "it would be of the greatest importance to finish the fight by early negotiation rather than by further military efforts, which will only result in more and more destruction and irreparable loss." "Yours is the sanest proposal that has been brought to this office in the last six months," said another Prime Minister.

The envoys were received by the following representatives of the belligerent nations:

Prime Minister Asquith and Foreign Minister Grey, in London.

Reichskanzler von Bethmann-Hollweg, and Foreign Minister von Jagow, in Berlin.

Prime Minister Stuergkh, Foreign Minister Burian, in Vienna; Prime Minister Tisza, in Budapest.

Prime Minister Salandra and Foreign Minister Sonino, in Rome.

Prime Minister Viviani and Foreign Minister Delcasse, in Paris.

Foreign Minister davignon, in Havre.

Foreign Minister Sasonoff, in Petrograd.

And by the following representatives of neutral governments:

Prime Minister Cort van der Linden and Foreign Minister Loudon, in The Hague.

Prime Minister Zahle and Foreign Minister Scavenius, in Copenhagen.

King Haakon, Prime Minister Knudsen, Foreign Minister Ihlen, and by Messrs. Loeyland, Asrstad Castberg and Jahren, the four presidents of the Storthing in Christiania.

Foreign Minister Wallenberg, in Stockholm.

President Motta and Foreign Minister Hoffman, in Berne.

President Wilson and Secretary of State Lansing in Washington.

While in Rome, the delegation went unofficially–that is to say, without a mandate from the Congress, to an audience with the Pope and the Cardinal Secretary of State.

As I recall those hurried journeys which Alice Hamilton and I made with Dr. Alletta Jacobs and her friend Madame Palthe to one warring country after another, it still seems marvelous to me that the people we met were so outspoken against war, with a freedom of expression which was not allowed later in any of the belligerent nations. Among certain young men, such as those editing the Cam-Magazine in Cambridge University, there was a veritable revolt against war and against the old men responsible for it who, they said, were "having field days on their own," in appealing to hate, intolerance and revenge without fear of contradiction from the younger generation.

We were impressed with the fact that in all countries the enthusiasm for continuing the war was largely fed on a fund of animosity growing out of the conduct of the war; England on fire over the atrocities in Belgium, Germany indignant over Englands blockade to starve her women and children. It seemed to us in our naivete, although it may be that we were not without a homely wisdom, that if the Press could be freed and an adequate offer of negotiations made, the war might be concluded before another winter of the terrible trench warfare. However, the three "envoys" from the United States, Emily Balch, Alice Hamilton and myself, wrote out our impressions as carefully as we were able in a little book, so that there is no use in repeating them here.

Shortly after our return the delegates from Holland, England and Austria met with us in the United States, and we issued what we called a manifesto, urging once more the calling of a Neutral Conference and giving our reasons therefor. This document is long since forgotten, lost in the stirring events which followed, although at the time it received a good deal of favorable comment, in the press of the neutral countries on both sides of the Atlantic, perhaps because it was difficult openly to oppose its modest recommendations. We were certainly well within the truth when we said that "we bear evidence of a rising desire and intention of vast companies of people in the neutral countries to turn a barren disinterestedness into an active goodwill. In Sweden, for example, more than 400 meetings were held in one day in different parts of the country, calling on the government to act.

"The excruciating burden of responsibility for the hopeless continuance of this war no longer rests on the will of the belligerent nations alone. It rests also on the will of those neutral governments and people who have been spared its shock but cannot, if they would, absolve themselves from their full share of responsibility for the continuance of war."

The first annual meeting of the Womens Peace Party was held at Washington in January, 1916. The reports showed that during the year mass meetings had been held all over the country, much material had been sent out from the central office for speeches arranged for by other public bodies, and in addition to the state branches there were one hundred and sixty-five group memberships, totaling about forty thousand women. In becoming a section of the Womens International Committee for Permanent Peace we were securely committed to an international body which at that time had well defined branches in fifteen countries.

The Congressional program adopted at the annual meeting included measures to oppose universal, compulsory, military service; to secure a joint commission to deal with problems arising between the United States and the Orient; and to formulate the principle that foreign investments shall be made without claim to military protection.

The third annual meeting was held at the end of eleven months, in December of 1916, again in Washington. The most important feature of it was a conference on Oppressed and Dependent Nationalities, arranged by Miss Grace Abbott, one of our members, who had had long experience as Superintendent of the Immigrant Protective League of Chicago.

The invitations to this special conference called attention to the fact that as Americans we believed that good government is no substitute for self-government, and that a federal form offers the most satisfactory method of giving local self-government in a country great in territory or complex in population. How Americas international policies might support or express these principles was the problem before the conference. It was believed that valuable advice could be given by those citizens of the United States who by their birth belonged to the dependent or oppressed nationalities and who, through their American experience, were familiar with the workings of our federal form of government.

Prominent representatives of the Poles, Czechoslovaks, Lithuanians and Letts, Ukrainians, Jugoslavs, Albanians, Armenians, Zionists and Irish Republicans were, for this reason, the speakers at the Conference. All the problems of conflicting claims and the creation of new subject minorities as a result of any territorial changes which might be made, were developed in the course of the Conference. Disagreement also developed as to the weight which should be given to historic claims in the righting of ancient wrongs in contrast to the demands of a present population.

This experimental conference had behind it a very sound theory of the contribution which American experience might have made toward a reconciliation of European differences in advance of the meeting of the Peace Conference. Professor Masaryk, later President of Czecho-Slo-vakia, attempted to accomplish such an end in the organization of the Central European nationalities, which actually came to a tentative agreement in Philadelphia more than a year later.

Had the federal form of government taken hold of the minds of the American representatives of various nationalities as strongly as did the desire for self-determination, or had the latter been coupled with an enthusiasm for federation, many of the difficulties inherent in the Peace Conference would have been anticipated. A federation among the succession states of Austria would have secured at the minimum a Customs Union and might have averted the most galling economic difficulties.

It was at this third annual meeting in Washington, the last held before the United States entered the war, that we discussed the inevitable shortage of food throughout the world which long-continued war entailed. For three years we, like many other sympathetic citizens of the United States, had been at times horribly oppressed with the consciousness that widespread famine had once more returned to the world. At moments there seemed to be no spot upon which to rest ones mind with a sense of well being. One recalled Serbia, where three-fourths of a million people out of the total population of three million, had perished miserably of typhus and other diseases superinduced by long continued privations; Armenia, where in spite of her heart-breaking history, famine and pestilence had never stalked so unchecked; Palestine, where the old horrors of the siege of Jerusalem, as described by Josephus, had been revived; and perhaps the crowning hor ror of all, the "Way of the Cross"–so called by the Russians because it was easily traced by the continuous crosses raised over the hastily dug graves–beginning with the Galician thoroughfares, and stretching south and east for fourteen hundred miles, upon which a distracted peasantry ran breathlessly until stopped by the Caspian Sea, or crossed the Ural Mountains into Asia, only to come back again because there was no food there.

We pointed out in our speeches what later became commonplace statements on hundreds of platforms, that although there had been universal bad harvests in 1916, the war itself was primarily responsible for the increasing dearth of food. Forty million men were in active army service, twenty million men and women were supporting the armies by their war activities, such as the manufacture of munitions, and perhaps as many more were in definite war industries, such as shipbuilding. Of course, not all these people were before the war directly engaged in producing food, but many of them were, and others were transporting or manufacturing it, and their wholesale withdrawal wrought havoc both in agriculture and in industry.

The European fields, worked by women and children and in certain sections by war prisoners, were lacking in fertilizers which could not be brought from remote ports nor be manufactured as usual in Europe, because nitrates and other such materials essential to ammunition were being diverted to that use. The U-boats constantly destroyed food-carrying ships, and many remote markets had become absolutely isolated, so that they could no longer contribute their food supplies to a hungry Europe.

Mr. Hoover, at the head of the American Relief Committee, was then feeding approximately 10,000,000 people in Belgium and northern France, but at that time little more was attempted in the feeding of civilian populations. Yet thousands of Americans were already finding this consciousness of starvation among European women and children increasingly hard to bear.

CHAPTER II.

THE NEUTRAL CONFERENCE PLUS THE FORD SHIP.

In the fall of 1915, after we had written our so-called "Manifesto," a meeting of the Womans Peace Party was called in New York City, at which we were obliged to make the discouraging report that, in spite of the fact that the accredited officials of the leading belligerent nations, namely, Great Britain, France, Russia, Belgium, Italy, Germany, Austria and Hungary, had expressed a willingness to cooperate in a Neutral Conference, and while the neutral nations, Norway, Sweden, Denmark, and Holland had been eager to participate in the proposed conference if it could be called by the United States, our own country was most reluctant. There seemed to us then to be two reasons for this reluctance; first that the United States could not call a neutral conference and ignore the South American countries, although to include even the largest of them would make too large a body, and secondly, that as the Central Powers had at that moment the technical military advantage, such a conference, if convened at all, should not be summoned until the military

situation was more balanced. We thought that we had adequately replied to both of these objections, but because of them or for other reasons President Wilson would not consider the proposition, nor was his attitude in the least changed later when one of our members came from a small European neutral country with the accredited proposition that her nation would call such a conference if it could be assured of the participation of the United States.

We seemed to have come to an impasse therefore, so far as calling a conference of neutrals was concerned unless we could bring to bear a tremendous pressure of public opinion upon the officials in Washington. The newspapers were, of course, closed to us so far as seriously advocating such a conference was concerned, although they were only too ready to seize upon any pretext which might make the effort appear absurd. We made one more attempt to induce the President to act, an attempt made possible through the generosity of Mrs. Henry Ford. She sent us a contribution of 5,000.00 which she afterwards increased to 8,000.00 and the entire sum was spent upon telegrams issued from New York and Chicago to eight thousand women, every one of whom was either the chairman or secretary of a womans organization, asking her to urge the President to call a conference of neutrals as an attempt to end the slaughter in Europe. These womens organizations included mutual benefit societies, all sorts of Church organizations, womens clubs and many others. The telegrams we sent averaged in cost 1.00 each. Of course we did not pay for the telegrams which we asked should be sent to President Wilson. He received about two thousand more than the number of our requests; they poured in at such a rate for three days that the office in Washington was obliged to engage two extra clerks who doubtless possessed the only pairs of eyes which ever saw the telegrams. Nevertheless, ten thousand womens organizations had learned that there was a project for a conference of neutrals and they had for a moment at least the comfort of knowing that a suggestion was being made which might result in arresting the bloodshed.

At this time an unexpected development gave the conference of neutrals only too much publicity and produced a season of great hilarity for the newspaper men of two continents. Madame Ro-sika Schwimmer, who still remained in the United States, had lectured in Detroit where she had been introduced to Mr. Henry Ford. For many months Mr. Ford had maintained a personal representative in Washington to keep him informed of possible openings for making peace with the understanding that such efforts "should not be mere talk nor education." During a long interview which Madame Schwimmer held with Mr. Ford and his wife, he expressed his willingness to finance the plan of a neutral conference and promised to meet her in New York in regard to it. He arrived in New York the very day the conference of the Womens Peace Party adjourned and he met with a small committee the same evening. Up to that moment all our efforts had been bent towards securing a conference supported by neutral governments who should send representatives to the body; but as it gradually became clear that the governments would not act, we hoped that a sum large enough to defray all the general expenses of such a conference might initiate it as a private enterprise.

It is easy to forget the state of the public mind at the end of the first year of the great war. At that moment much was said in regard to the unwillingness of both sides to "dig in" for another winter of trench warfare, and a statement was constantly repeated that, on the western front alone during an average day when no military position had been changed, the loss was still three thousand men. We knew how concerned the responsible statesmen in each country were about this destruction of young life, and there were many proofs that the very sense of modern efficiency so carefully fostered in one industrial coun try after another, was steadily being outraged. The first Christmas of the war the Pope had made a touching, although futile appeal for a cessation of hostilities; it might be possible that as the second Christmas approached, mens minds would be open to a proposition looking towards the gradual substitution of adjudication for military methods. It is very difficult after five years of war to recall the attitude of most normal people during those first years. Such people had not yet acknowledged the necessity and propriety of war, their mental processes were not yet so inhibited but that many of them still believed that it might be possible to clarify the atmosphere, and to find a way out of the desperate situation in which Europe found itself. At least the beginnings of a solution might be found by the constant exercise of such judgment as carefully selected men from the neutral countries might be able to bring to bear. Such a conference sitting continuously would take up one possibility after another for beginning peace negotiations. It was further hoped by the most sanguine that such a conference, if successful, might undertake the international administration of the territory conquered by either side until its final disposition was determined upon; thus the allied side would turn over to it the German colonies in South Africa, the Central Powers such parts of Belgium and North ern France as they then occupied, and Russia the portions of Galicia she was then holding. At the end of the war there would be in actual operation an international body similar to that constituted at Algeciras or to that since advocated by the League of Nations in regard to the determination of mandates. It would be developed into the beginnings of a de facto international government. It might bring hope to certain soldiers on both sides of the conflict who were confessedly fighting on doggedly day after day because they saw no one able to detach them from it. There were thousands of "loyal" Americans who in 1915 sincerely wished to see the carnage stopped and Europe once more reconstructed; they knew that the longer the war lasted the harder it would be to make peace and that each monthof war inevitably tended to involve more nations. They were amazed at the futile efforts of European statesmen, at their willingness and at moments their apparent eagerness to hand their functions over to military men, and at their craven acceptance as inevitable of much which might conceivably be changed. Many people went about day after day with an oppressive sense of the horrible disaster which had befallen the world and woke up many times during the night as from a hideous nightmare. Men must have felt like this during the time of pestilence, in the fourteenth century for instance, when the bubonic plague destroyed about thirty-five million people in Europe, and no determined and intelligent effort was made to stop it. The youth in many of the belligerent countries had been sent to war by men put in office through slight majorities won in elections based upon purely domestic issues. Yet here they were at the behest and determination of the men thus elected, often against their own convictions and instincts, ranged against each other in long-drawn battle with but one inevitable issue. There must be a residuum of kindliness and good sense somewhere in the world! It was customary at that time to ask the opponent of war what he would have done had he been in France when the German war machine threatened her very existence. We could only reply that we were not criticizing France, that we had every admiration for her gallant courage, but that what we were urging at that moment was the cessation of hostilities and the substitution of another method. Was a group of men living in Prussia, who had urged the development and perfection of a military machine which, from the very nature of the case must in the course of time be put into operation, to be allowed to determine the future of all the young men in Europe? Would not the system of conscription, spread to England and her colonies overseas, but increase the practice of militarism?

Our hopes were high that evening in New York as we talked over the possible men and a few women from the Scandinavian countries, from Holland and Switzerland, who possessed the international mind and might lend themselves to the plan of a neutral conference. We were quite worldly enough to see that we should have to begin with some well-known Americans, but we were confident that at least a half dozen of them with whom we had already discussed the plan, would be ready to go. Mr. Ford took a night train to Washington to meet an appointment with President Wilson, perhaps still hoping that the plan might receive some governmental sanction and at least wishing to be assured that, as a private enterprise, it would not embarrass the government.

During the day, as I went about New York in the interest of other affairs and as yet saying nothing of the new plan, it seemed to me that perhaps it was in character that the effort from the United States should be initiated not by the government but by a self-made business man who approached the situation from a purely human point of view, almost as a working man would have done. On the evening after his return from Washington Mr. Ford reported that the President had declared him quite within his rights in financing a neutral conference and had wished all success to the enterprise.

The difficulties, however, began that very evening when Mr. Ford asked his business agent to show us the papers which chartered the Norwegian boat Oscar II for her next trans-Atlantic voyage. Some of the people attending the committee meeting-evidently knew of this plan, but I was at once alarmed, insisting that it would be easy enough for the members of the conference to travel to Stockholm or The Hague by various steamship lines, paying their own expenses; that we needed Mr. Fords help primarily in organizing a conference but not in transporting the people. Mr. Fords response was to the effect that the more publicity the better and that the sailing of the ship itself would make known the conference more effectively than any other method could possibly do. After that affairs moved rapidly. Mr. Louis Lochner came on from Chicago to act as secretary to the undertaking, which was established with its own headquarters in New York. An attempt the very first day to organize a committee who should be responsible for selecting the personnel of the conference proved difficult. Mr. Ford himself was eager to issue the invitations and had begun with two of his oldest and best friends, John Burroughs and Thomas A. Edison. At the very first, a group of college young people presented a list of students, limited to two from each of the leading colleges and universities whom they wished to have invited. We pointed out that these could hardly hope to be of direct value to the conference itself, but it was hard to set aside the reply that what was needed was not only efforts at adjudication by a well-considered conference of elders but also the warmth and reassurance which youth would bring to the enterprise. The youthful advocates also believed that their demonstration might evoke a compunction among the elderly statesmen responsible for the war who, by calling any such remonstrance treason, had absolutely inhibited pacifist youth in Europe from expression of opinion. There was also much feeling at the moment among certain students in American universities over the suppression in England of the Cambridge Magazine whose editorial policy had been consistently anti-military, and over the fact that Bertrand Russell had been asked to resign from Cambridge University.

A college group was finally invited and later proved a somewhat embarrassing factor in the enterprise. I left for Chicago before the flood of invitations were sent; many of them were addressed to honest, devoted, and also distinguished people, although the offer of a crusading journey to Europe with all expenses paid could but attract many fanatical and impecunious reformers.

Almost immediately upon my return to Chicago, ten days before the Oscar II sailed, the newspaper accounts from New York began to be most disquieting. We had not expected any actual cooperation from the newspapers, but making all allowances for that, the enterprise seemed to be exhibiting unfortunate aspects. The conference itself was seldom mentioned, but the journey and the ship were made all important and mysterious people with whom Madame Schwim-mer was said to be in communication, were constantly featured. The day when Mr. Fords slogan "Get the Boys out of the trenches by Christmas" was spread all over the front pages of the dailies I spent large sums of money, telephoning to the secretary in New York begging him to keep to the enterprise in hand, which I reminded him was the conference of neutrals. Having so recently traveled in Europe under wartime regulations, I knew that such propaganda would be considered treasonable and put the enterprise in a very dangerous position. Mr. Lochner reminded me of Mr. Fords well-known belief that direct appeal to the "the boys" was worth much more than the roundabout educational methods we were advocating. Almost simultaneously with this untoward development the secretary received the resignations of three leading internationalists who had seriously considered going, and of two others who had but recently accepted. They had all been convinced of the possible usefulness of a conference of neutrals, at least to the extent of giving "continuous mediation" a trial, but they had become absolutely disconcerted by the extraneous developments of the enterprise. On the other hand, the people in New York in charge of the enterprise believed that the anti-war movement throughout its history had been too quiet-istic and much too grey and negative; that the heroic aspect of life had been too completely handed over to war, leaving pacifists under the suspicion that they cared for safety first and cherished survival above all else; that a demonstration was needed, even a spectacular one to show that ardor and comradeship were exhibited by the non-militarists as well; in fact, it was the pacifists who believed that life itself was so glorious an adventure that the youth of one nation had no right to deprive the youth of another nation of their share in it; that living itself, which all youth had in common, was larger and more inclusive than the nationalistic differences so unfairly stressed by their elders.

I was fifty-five years old in 1915; I had already "learned from life," to use Dantes great phrase, that moral results are often obtained through the most unexpected agencies; that it is very easy to misjudge the value of an undertaking by a critical or unfair estimate of the temperament and ability of those undertaking it. It was quite possible that with Mr. Fords personal knowledge of the rank and file of working men he had shrewdly interpreted the situation, that he understood the soldier who was least responsible for the war and could refuse to continue only if the appeal came simultaneously to both sides. The bulk of the soldiers in every army are men who ordinarily work with their hands in industry, in transportation and in agriculture. We had been told, only the month before, of the response on the part of the English soldiers when governmental officials had been sent to France to go through the trenches in order to find skilled mechanics to work in the arsenals and munition factories which had been found to be such an important factor in modern warfare. How eagerly the men confessed, when there was no question of lack of patriotism involved, that they had longed for the feel of tools in their hands, that they had felt disconnected and unhappy. Possibly what Mr. Veblen calls "the instinct of workmanship" asserted itself in mute but powerful rebellion through their very muscles and nerves against the work of destruction to which their skilled hands were set. Was the appeal which Mr. Ford was making more natural and normal, more fitted to the situation than that which we had so eagerly been advocating? At any rate the situation was taken quite out of the hands of the original promoters, for among other things which Mr. Ford had gained from his wide experience was an overwhelming belief in the value of advertising; even derision was better than no "story" at all. Partly in pursuance of this policy, partly because they themselves were clamorous, no fewer than sixty-four newspaper men finally sailed on the Oscar II.

During the days of my preparation for the journey, which was largely an assembling of warm clothing, for there was little fuel in the Scandinavian countries even then and we were to land in December, I tried to make my position clear to remonstrating friends. Admitting the plan had fallen into the hands of Mr. Ford who had long taken an inexplicable position in regard to peace propaganda, and that with many notable exceptions, a group of very eccentric people had attached themselves to the enterprise, so that there was every chance for a fiasco, I still felt committed to it and believed that at the worst it would be a protest from the rank and file of America, young and old, learned and simple, against the continuation of the war which in Europe was more and more being then regarded as inevitable. I was so convinced of the essential soundness of the conference of neutrals and so confident of European participation, that I was inclined to consider the sensational and unfortunate journey of the American contingent as a mere incident to the undertaking, for after all the actual foundations of the conference itself would have to be laid on the other side of the Atlantic. It became clearer every day that whoever became associated with the ship would be in for much ridicule and social opprobrium, but that of course seemed a small price to pay for a protest against war. Even in Mr. Fords much repeated slogan to "come out of the trenches" there was a touch of what might be called the Christian method, "cease to do evil," you yourself, just where you are, whatever the heads of the church and state may dictate. Whole pages of Tolstoys reaction to the simple Christian teaching raced through my mind; was this slogan a slangy 20th century version of the same decisive appeal?

What my interpretation of the enterprise would have been, had I become part of it, is of course impossible to state, for on the eve of leaving home, a serious malady which had pursued me from childhood reappeared and I was lying in a hospital bed in Chicago not only during the voyage of the Oscar II, but during the following weeks when the Neutral Conference was actually established in Stockholm.

It is useless to speculate on what might have occurred at various times but for our physical limitations; we must, perforce, accommodate ourselves to them, and it is never easy, although I had had the training which comes to a child with "spinal disease," as it was called in my youth.

Madame Schwimmer, who, as a journalist and suffrage organizer, had had wide experience in many European countries outside of Hungary, was convinced that the neutral conference would not succeed unless it had back of it the imaginative interest of the common people throughout Europe. She therefore arranged that formal receptions should be accorded to the party in the four neutral countries of Norway, Sweden, Denmark and Holland. The entire expedition, so far as she conducted it, was in the grand manner for she believed, rightly or wrongly, that the drooping Peace Movement needed the prestige and reassurance that such a policy would bring to it. Unfortunately the policy exposed her both to the charge of extravagance and of having manufactured a claque.

Difficulties developed during the journey; Mr. Ford left a few days after the group arrived in Norway, in the midst of journalistic misrepresentations and Madame Schwimmer resigned from the Conference, during the early months of its existence. But in spite of disasters the Neutral Conference was finally set up at Stockholm, on January 26, 1916, after the Burgomaster of the city had introduced an interpellation in the Rikstag, of which he was a member, asking the Swedish Government to define its attitude on neutral mediation.

Gradually the personnel was completed by five representatives each from Denmark, Holland, Norway, Sweden and Switzerland, with three from the United States. Among the Europeans were Professors of International Law, of Economics, of Philosophy, the legal advisor to the Nobel Institute, men and women who were officers of National Peace Societies, members of Parliament and city officials. They first issued a carefully considered appeal addressed "To the Governments and Parliaments of the Neutral Nations represented at the second Hague Conference" begging them to offer official mediation, and quoting from The Hague Conventions to show that such an offer could not be construed as an unfriendly act.

This appeal was given general publicity by the European Press, even in the belligerent countries, and at least served to draw attention once more to the fact that a continuation of the war was not necessarily inevitable. Resolutions based on the appeal were considered by three National Parliaments, and the appeal itself was discussed at a formal meeting of the Prime Ministers of the three Scandinavian countries.

At Easter, 1916, the Conference issued an appeal to "The Governments, Parliaments and People of Belligerent Nations." This was the result of much study, and was founded upon an intelligent effort to obtain the various nationalistic points of view. An enormous correspondence on the subject had taken place, and representatives of many nationalities had appeared before the Conference; these ranged from the accredited governmental officials to the Esthonian peasant who came on skiis, many miles over the ice and snow, crossing the frontier at the risk of his life, not daring even to tell his name, and wishing the bare fact of his appearance to be suppressed, until he should have had time to return to his own country. He added one more to the tragic petitions, received from all parts of Europe. This official appeal to the belligerent nations, foreshadowing the famous fourteen points, was also widely published.

The Conference of Neutrals, reorganized into an International Commission devoted to promoting the public opinion necessary for a lasting peace whenever the governments should be ready to act, had much to do with stimulating general meetings held in all the neutral countries on Hague Day, May 18th, and again on the second anniversary of the war in August. George Brandes of Denmark, wrote a stirring appeal for Peace, as did the poets and writers of various countries, including Ellen Key and Selma Lagerlof. For the moment a demand for the cessation of the war be came vocal, at least in those countries where such demands were not officially suppressed.

Because the beginning of actual mediation, founded upon visits between citizens from the belligerent nations with those from the neutral must of necessity be conducted quietly, the Conference finally left two of its members in each of the five neutral countries, with its headquarters at The Hague, where the two delegates from the United States were established.

When Louis Lochner came back to the United States in October, 1916, he was able to give an enthusiastic report. He arrived in the midst of the "he kept us out of war" Presidential campaign. The Democratic Party in the very convention which re-nominated President Wilson and drew the Party Platform, had endorsed a Leagus of Nations policy. Mr. Lochner reported that even the Germans were ready for international disarmament, and that the question on everybodys lips was "how soon will Wilson act?" We were sure that Mr. Wilson would act in his own best way, and were most anxious not to take the attitude towards him by which the Abolitionist so constantly embarrassed President Lincoln during the Civil War.

Mr. Ford at that time was guaranteeing to the Conference a steady income of ten thousand dollars a month, the first difficulties had subsided and the movement was constantly gaining prestige. The Norway delegation, for instance, then consisting of Christian Lange, general secretary of the Interparliamentary Union; Dr. Horgenstierne, president of the University of Christiania, and Haakon Loeken, states attorney for Christiania. This personnel was not unlike that of the other countries.

On December 10, 1916, President Wilson issued his famous Peace Note, and it seemed as if at last the world were breathing another air. For the time being the pacifists were almost popular, or at least felt a momentary lift of the curious strain which inevitably comes to him who finds himself differing with every one about him.

In January of 1917, Mr. Lochner returned again to the United States in company with the man who had been engaged in negotiations with Great Britain, and saw the President twice. I was ill and confined to my room at this time. But in a long conversation which I had with Mr. Lochner in Chicago, as he reported recent interviews with Mr. Ford and his secretaries, it was evident that the benefactor of the Neutral Conference was reflecting the change in public opinion, and like many another pacifist, who does not believe in war as such, was nevertheless making an exception of "this war." In February Mr. Fords changed position was unmistakable. He an nounced that he would give no more support to the European undertaking after March first, and he withdrew from the Neutral Conference plan almost as abruptly as he had entered it.

Thus came to an end all our hopes for a Conference of Neutrals devoted to continuous mediation. Our womens organizations as such had had nothing to do with the "Ford Ship," but of course we had assiduously urged the Conference which it was designed to serve, and our members in many countries had promoted the de facto Conference. Certainly no one could justly charge us with "passivity" in our efforts to secure it.

During my long days of invalidism in California the following spring, I had plenty of time to analyze the situation. Had we been over-persistent, so eager for the grapes that we were willing to gather thistles, had our identification with the sensational Peace Ship been an exhibition of moral daring or merely an example of woeful lack of judgment? When I contrasted the Ford undertaking with another International Peace Movement absolutely free from any sensationalism, I found that the latter had been scarcely more successful: The Minimum Program Committee had been supported by pacifists from many countries. It was inaugurated in the spring of 1915 at a conference composed of distinguished men and women held at The Hague, where it established perman ent headquarters. It had put forward a rational program, and had kept alive the hopes for an ordered world, functioning throughout the war and for two years following with no act of indiscretion. It was, in fact, so cautious that at a dinner in New York which I attended as a member of the American Committee of 100, certain officers, alarmed at the remote connection with the Ford Ship which Mr. Lochners presence there indicated, asked him to resign. To them, as to so many millions of their fellow citizens, the slogan that "this is a war to end war" and the hope that the Peace Commission would provide for an enduring peace, were convincing. They did not realize how old the slogan was, nor how many times it had lured men into condoning war.

California also afforded time for reading books in which it was easy to discover that never had so much been said about bringing war to an end forevermore, as by the group of Allied Nations who waged the last campaign against Napoleon. They declared in the grandiloquent phrases they used so easily that their aims were "the reconstruction of the moral order," "a regeneration of the political system of Europe," and "the establishment of an enduring peace founded upon a just redistribution of political forces." But Napoleon was "crushed" and none of their moral hopes were fulfilled. They too were faced at the end of the war, as are the victors and vanquished of every war, by unimaginable suffering, by economic ruin, by the irreparable loss of thousands of young men, by the set back of orderly progress.

As the Great War incredibly continued year after year, as the entrance of one nation after another increased the number of young combatants, as the war propaganda grew ever more bitter and irrational, there were moments when we were actually grateful for every kind of effort we had made. At such times, the consciousness of social opprobrium, of having become an easy mark for the cheapest comment, even the sense of frustration were, I am certain, easier to bear than would have been the consciousness that in our fear of sensationalism we had left one stone unturned to secure the Conference of Neutrals which seemed at least to us a possible agency for shortening the conflict.

CHAPTER III.

PRESIDENT WILSONS POLICIES AND THE WOMENS PEACE PARTY

We heard with much enthusiasm the able and discriminating annual message delivered by the President in December, 1915. It seemed to lay clearly before the country "the American strategy" which the President evidently meant to carry out; he had called for a negotiated peace in order to save both sides from utter exhaustion and moral disaster in the end. We were all disappointed that when he asked for a statement of war aims both sides were reluctant to respond, but Germanys flat refusal put her at an enormous disadvantage and enabled the President in his role of leading neutral to appeal to the German people over the heads of their rulers with terms so liberal that it was hoped that the people themselves would force an end to the war. Naturally, a plea for a negotiated peace could only be addressed to the liberals throughout the world, who were probably to be found in every country involved in the conflict. If the strategy had succeeded these liberals would have come into power in all the parliamen tary countries and the making of the peace as well as the organization of the international body to be formed after the war, would naturally have been in liberal hands. The peace conference itself would inevitably have been presided over by the President of the great neutral nation who had forced the issue. All this in sharp contrast to what would result if the United States, with its enormous resources, entered into the war, for if the war were carried on to a smashing victory, the "bitter enders" would inevitably be in power at its conclusion.

We also counted upon the fact that this great war had challenged the validity of the existing status between nations, as it had never been questioned before, and that radical changes were being proposed by the most conservative of men everywhere. As conceived by the pacifist, the constructive task laid upon the United States at that moment was the discovery of an adequate moral basis for a new relationship between nations. The exercise of the highest political Intelligence might hasten to a speedy completion for immediate use that international organization which had been so long discussed and so ardently anticipated.

Pacifists believed that in the Europe of 1914,. certain tendencies were steadily pushing towards large changes which in the end made war, because the system of peace had no way of effecting those changes without war, no adequate international organization which could cope with the situation. The conception of peace founded upon the balance of power or the undisturbed status quo, was so negative that frustrated national impulses and suppressed vital forces led to war, because no method of orderly expression had been devised.

The world was bent on a change, for it knew that the real denial and surrender of life is not physical death but acquiescence in hampered conditions and unsolved problems. Agreeing substantially with this analysis of the causes of the war, we pacifists, so far from passively wishing nothing to be done, contended on the contrary that this world crisis should be utilized for the creation of an international government able to make the necessary political and economic changes which were due; we felt that it was unspeakably stupid that the nations should fail to create an international organization through which each one, without danger to itself, might recognize and even encourage the impulse toward growth in other nations.

In spite of many assertions to the contrary, we were not advocating the mid-Victorian idea that good men from every country meet together at The Hague or elsewhere, there to pass a resolution that "wars hereby cease" and that "the world hereby be federated." What we insisted upon was that the world could be organized politically by its statesmen as it had been already organized into an international fiscal system by its bankers. We asked why the problem of building a railroad to Bagdad, of securing corridors to the sea for a land-locked nation, or warm water harbors for Russia, should result in war. Surely the minds of this generation were capable of solving such problems as the minds of other generations had solved their difficult problems. Was it not obvious that such situations transcended national boundaries and must be approached in a spirit of world adjustment, that they could not be peacefully adjusted while mens minds were still held apart by national suspicions and rivalries.

The pacifists hoped that the United States might perform a much needed service in the international field, by demonstrating that the same principles of federation and of an interstate tribunal might be extended among widely separated nations, as they had already been established between our own contiguous states. Founded upon the great historical experiment of the United States, it seemed to us that American patriotism might rise to a supreme effort because her own experience for more than a century had so thoroughly committed her to federation and to peaceful adjudication as matters of every-day government. The Presidents speech before the Senate embodied such a masterly restatement of early American principles that thousands of his fellow citizens dedicated themselves anew to finding a method for applying them in the wider and more difficult field of international relationships. We were stirred to enthusiasm by certain indications that President Wilson was preparing for this difficult piece of American strategy.

It was early in January, 1916, that the President put forth his Pan-American program before the Pan-American Scientific Congress which was held in Washington at that time. His first point, "to unite in guaranteeing to each other absolute political independence and territorial integrity" was not so significant to us as the second, "to settle all disputes arising between us by investigation and arbitration."

One of our members had been prominently identified with this Congress. I had addressed its Womans Auxiliary and at our Executive Committee meeting, held in January, 1916, we felt that we had a right to consider the Administration committed still further to the path of arbitration upon which it had entered in September, 1914, when treaties had been signed in Washington with Great Britain, France, Spain and China, each providing for commissions of inquiry in cases of difficulty. Secretary Bryan had stated at that time that twenty-six nations had already signed such treaties, and that Russia, Germany and Austria were being urged to do so. Then there had been the Presidents Mexican policy which, in spite of great pressure had kept the United States free from military intervention, and had been marked by great forebearance to a sister republic which as yet was struggling awkwardly toward self-government.

But it was still early in 1916 that the curious and glaring difference between the Presidents statement of foreign policy and the actual bent of the Administration began to appear. In the treaty with Haiti, ratified by the United States Senate in February, 1916, the United States guaranteed Haiti territorial and political independence and in turn was empowered to administer Haitis customs and finances for twenty years. United States Marines, however, had occupied Haiti since a riot which had taken place in 1915 and had set up a military government, including a strict military censorship. All sorts of stories were reaching the office of the Womans Peace Party, some of them from white men wearing the United States uniform, some of them from black men in despair over the treatment accorded to the island by "armed invaders." We made our protest to Washington, Miss Breckenridge presenting the protest in person after she had made a most careful investigation into all the records to be found in the possession of the government. She received a most evasive reply having to do with a naval base which the United States had established there in preference to allowing France or Germany to do so. In response to our suggestion that the whole matter be referred to the Central American Court we were told that the Court was no longer functioning, and a little later indeed the Carnegie building itself was dismantled, thus putting an end to one of the most promising beginnings of international arbitration.

In February, 1916, came the Nicaraguan treaty including among other things the payment of 3,-000,000 for a naval base, seemingly in contradiction to the Presidents former stand in regard to Panama Canal tolls and the fortification of the Canal. Again the information given in response to the inquiry of the Womans Peace Party was frag-mentary and again responsibility seemed to be divided between several departments of the government.

In the late summer of the same year there came the purchase of the Virgin Islands from Denmark. A plebiscite had been taken in Denmark in regard to this sale but none was to be taken on the islands themselves that the people living there might say whether or not they wished to be transferred. When the Womans Peace Party urged such a plebiscite, we were told that there was no doubt that the Virgin Islands people did wish such a transfer, but there was no reply to our contention that it would make it all the easier therefore, to take the vote, and that the situation offered a wonderful opportunity actually to put into practice on a small scale what the President himself would shortly ask Europe to do on a large scale. This opportunity, of course, was never utilized and thousands of people were transferred from one government to another without a formal expression of their wishes.

In November, 1916, military occupation of the San Dominican Republic was proclaimed by Captain Knapp of the United States Navy and a military government was established there under control of the United States. Again we made our protest but this time as a matter of form, having little hope of a satisfactory reply although we were always received with much official courtesy. We were quite ready to admit that the government was pursuing a consistent policy in regard to the control of the Caribbean Sea, but we not only felt the danger of using the hunt for naval bases as an excuse to subdue one revolution after another and to set up military government, but also very much dreaded the consequences of such a line of action upon the policy of the United States in its larger international relationships. We said to each other and once when the occasion of fered, to the President himself, that to reduce the theory to action was the only way to attract the attention of a world at war; Europe would be convinced of the sincerity of the United States only if the President was himself actually carrying out his announced program in the Caribbean or wherever opportunity offered. Out of the long international struggle had arisen a moral problem the solution of which could only be suggested through some imperative act which would arrest attention as a mere statement could not possibly do. It seemed to us at moments as if the President were imprisoned in his own spacious intellectuality, and had forgotten the overwhelming value of the deed.

Up to the moment of his nomination for a second term our hopes had gradually shifted to the belief that the President would finally act, not so much from his own preferences or convictions, but from the impact upon him of public opinion, from the momentum of the pressure for Peace, which we were sure the campaign itself would make clear to him. I was too ill at that time for much campaigning but knew quite well that my vote could but go to the man who had been so essentially right in international affairs. I held to this position through many spirited talks with Progressive friends who felt that our mutual hopes could be best) secured through other parties, and as I grew better, and was able to undertake a minimum of speaking and writing, it was all for President Wilsons reelection and for an organization of a League of Nations. My feeble efforts were recognized beyond their desert when, after the successful issue in November I was invited to a White House dinner tendered to a few people who had been the Presidents steadfast friends.

The results of the campaign had been very gratifying to the members of our group. It seemed at last as if peace were assured and the future safe in the hands of a chief executive who had received an unequivocal mandate from the people "to keep us out of war." We were, to be sure, at moments a little uneasy in regard to his theory of self-government, a theory which had reappeared in his campaign speeches and was so similar to that found in his earlier books. It seemed at those times as if he were not so eager for a mandate to carry out the will of the people as for an opportunity to lead the people whither in his judgment their best interest lay. Did he place too much stress on leadership?

But moments of uneasiness were forgotten and the pacifists in every part of the world were not only enormously reassured but were sent up into the very heaven of internationalism, as it were, when President Wilson delivered his famous speech to the Senate in January, 1917, which forecast his fourteen points. Some of these points had, of course, become common property among Liberals since the first year of the war when they had been formulated by The League for Democratic Control in England and later became known as a "union" program. Our Womans International Congress held at The Hague in May, 1915, had incorporated most of the English formula and had added others. The President himself had been kind enough to say when I presented our Hague program to him in August, 1915, that they were the best formulation he had seen up to that time.

President Wilson, however, later not only gathered together the best liberal statements yet made, formulated them in his incomparable English and added others of his own, but he was the first responsible statesman to enunciate them as an actual program for guidance in a troubled world. Among the thousands of congratulatory telegrams received by the President at that time none could have been more enthusiastic than those sent officially and personally by the members of our little group. We considered that the United States was committed not only to using its vast neutral power to extend democracy throughout the world, but also to the conviction that democratic ends could not be attained through the technique of war. In short, we believed that rational thinking and rea sonable human relationships were once more publicly recognized as valid in international affairs.

If, after the declaration of his foreign policy, it seemed to our group that desire and achievement were united in one able protagonist, the philosopher become king, so to speak this state of mind was destined to be short lived, for almost immediately the persistent tendency of the President to divorce his theory from the actual conduct of state affairs threw us into a state of absolute bewilderment. During a speaking tour in January, 1917, he called attention to the need of a greater army, and in St. Louis openly declared that the United States should have the biggest navy in the world.

We were in despair a few weeks later when in Washington the President himself led the Preparedness parade and thus publicly seized the leadership of the movement which had been started and pushed by his opponents. It was an able political move if he believed that the United States should enter the European conflict through orthodox warfare, but he had given his friends every right to suppose that he meant to treat the situation through a much bolder and at the same time more subtle method. The question with us was not one of national isolation, although we were constantly told that this was the alternative to war, it was purely a question of the method the United States should take to enter into a world situation. The crisis, it seemed to us, offered a test of the vigor and originality of a nation whose very foundations were laid upon a willingness to experiment.

It was at this time that another disconcerting factor in the situation made itself felt; a factor which was brilliantly analyzed in Randolph Bournes article entitled "War and the Intellectuals." The article was a protest against the "unanimity with which the American intellectuals had thrown their support to the use of war technique in the crisis in which America found herself," and against "the riveting of the war mind upon a hundred million more of the worlds people." It seemed as if certain intellectuals, editors, professors, clergymen, were energetically pushing forward the war against the hesitation and dim perception of the mass of the people. They seemed actually to believe that " a war free from any taint of self-seeking could secure the triumph of democracy and internationalize the world." They extolled the President as a great moral leader because he was irrevocably leading the country into war. The long established peace societies and their orthodox organs quickly fell into line expounding the doctrine that the worlds greatest war was to make an end to all wars. It was hard for some of us to understand upon what experi ence this pathetic belief in the regenerative results of war could be founded; but the world had become filled with fine phrases and this one, which afforded comfort to many a young soldier, was taken up and endlessly repeated with an entire absence of the critical spirit.

Through the delivery of the second inaugural address the President continued to stress the reconstruction of the world after the war as the aim of American diplomacy and endeavor. Certainly his pacifist friends had every right to believe that he meant to attain this by newer and finer methods than those possible in warfare, but it is only fair to say that his words were open to both constructions.

It will always be difficult to explain the change in the Presidents intention (if indeed it was a change) occurring between his inaugural address on March 4th and his recommendation for a declaration of war presented to Congress on April 2nd. A well known English economist has recently written: "The record shows Mr. Wilson up to 1917 essentially a pacifist, and assailed as such. There is nothing in the external evidence to explain his swift plunge into materialism. His too proud to fight maxim was repeated after the Lusi-tania incident. There is no evidence that the people who had elected him in the previous fall because he had kept us out wanted to go in until Mr. Wilson made them want. Why did he? What was the rapid conversion which it is commonly supposed Mr. Wilson underwent in the winter of 1916-1917?"

The pacifists were not idle during these days. A meeting of all the leading peace societies was called in New York in March and a committee of five, of which two were members of the Womans Peace Party, was appointed to wait upon the President with suggestions for what we ventured to call possible alternatives to war. Professor Hull of Swarthmore College, a former student of the Presidents, presented a brief resume of what other American presidents had done through adjudication when the interests of American shipping had become involved during European wars; notably, George Washington during the French Revolution and John Adams in the Napoleonic War, so that international adjudication instituted by Chief Justice Jay became known in Europe as "the American plan." The President was, of course, familiar with that history, as he reminded his old pupil, but he brushed it aside as he did the suggestion that if the attack on American shipping were submitted to The Hague tribunal, it might result in adjudication of the issues of the great war itself. The Labor man on the committee still expressed the hope for a popular referendum before war should be de clared, and we once more pressed for a conference of neutrals. Other suggestions were presented by a committee from the Union Against Militarism who entered the Presidents office as we were leaving it. The Presidents mood was stern and far from the scholars detachment as he told us of recent disclosures of German machinations in Mexico and announced the impossibility of any form of adjudication. He still spoke to us, however, as to fellow pacifists to whom he was forced to confess that war had become inevitable. He used one phrase which I had heard Colonel House use so recently that it still stuck firmly in my memory. The phrase was to the effect that, as head of a nation participating in the war, the President of the United States would have a seat at the Peace Table, but that if he remained the representative of a neutral country he could at best only "call through a crack in the door." The appeal he made was, in substance, that the foreign policy which we so extravagantly admired could have a chance If he were there to push and to defend them, but not otherwise. It was as if his hearts desire spoke through his words and dictated his view of the situation. But I found my mind challenging his whole theory of leadership. Was it a result of my bitter disappointment that I hotly and no doubt unfairly asked myself whether any man had the right to rate his moral leadership so high that he could consider the sacrifice of the lives of thousands of his young countrymen a necessity? I also reminded myself that all the study of modern social science is but a revelation of the fallacy of such a point of view, a discrediting of the Carlyle contention that the people must be led into the ways of righteousness by the experience, acumen and virtues of the great man. It was possible that the President would "go to the people" once more as he had gone years before with a brilliant formulization of democracy in education when he wanted his Princeton policy confirmed; or as he had appealed to the peace loving people during his campaign, solely in order to confirm what he wanted to do and to explain what he thought wise. In neither case had he offered himself as a willing instrument to carry out the peoples desires. He certainly did not dig the channels through which their purposes might flow and his own purpose be obtained because it had become one with theirs. It seemed to me quite obvious that the processes of war would destroy more democratic institutions than he could ever rebuild however much he might declare the purpose of war to be the extension of democracy. What was this curious break between speech and deed, how could he expect to know the doctrine if he refused to do the will?

Some of us felt that this genuine desire on the part of the President, to be in a position to do great good was perhaps the crux of the difficulty later when he actually took his place at the Peace Table, sitting in fact at the head of a table, at which no umpire could have taken a seat, since only those on one side of the great conflict were permitted to sit there. The President had a seat at the Peace Table as one among other victors, not as the impartial adjudicator. He had to drive a bargain for his League of Nations, he could not insist upon it as the inevitable basis for negotiations between two sides, the foundation of a "peace between equals."

Were the difficulties of the great compromise inherent in the situation, and would they still have been there even if both sides had been present at a conference presided over by a fair minded judge? Certainly some of the difficulties would have yielded in such an atmosphere and some of the mistakes would have been averted. Twenty-six governments of the world stood convicted of their own impotence to preserve life and property, they were directly responsible for the loss of ten million men in military service, as many more people through the disease and desolation following war, for the destruction of untold accumulations of civilized life. What would have been the result had the head of one nation been there to testify to a new standard in national government? What might have happened if President Wilson could have said in January, 1919, what he had said in January, 1917,–"A victors terms imposed upon the vanquished. would leave a sting, a resentment, a bitter memory upon which terms of peace would rest not permanently but only as upon quicksand," or again, "The right state of mind, the right feeling between nations, is as necessary for a lasting peace as is the just settlement of vexed questions of territory, or of racial and national allegiance." At that very moment the wind of idealism was blowing strongly across Europe, there were exaggerated hopes of a new and better world from which war should be forever banished. Europe distrusted any compromise with a monster which had already devoured her young men and all but destroyed her civilization. A man who had stood firmly against participation in war could have had his way with the common people in every country. The President became the center of the worlds hopes because of the things he had said against war, and because people believed that he expressed their own abhorrence. Did the League of Nations fail to win their hearts not because it was too idealistic or too pacifistic but because it permitted war in too many instances, because its very structure and functioning is pervaded by the war spirit, the victorious disciplin ing the defeated, whereas the people had dreamed of a League of Peace lifting up all those who had been the victims of militarism?

General Smuts has said that the Paris Peace in destroying the moral idealism born of the sacrifices of the war, did almost as much as the war itself to shatter the structure of western civilization. But the disastrous Peace came about, to quote the words of General Smuts himself, because "in the end not only the leaders but the people themselves preferred a bit of booty here, a strategic frontier there, a coal field or an oil well, an addition to their population or their resources–to all the faint allurements of an ideal." It was indeed the human spirit itself which failed, but the human spirit under a temptation which an earlier peace might have diminished. An impartial judge who could have insisted that there should be "no discriminations to those to whom we wish to be just, and those to whom we do not wish to be just," might in a measure have cooled the nationalistic passions inevitably aroused by a long and disastrous war, might have substituted other hopes for those so long deferred, for the glittering promises which must of necessity remain unfulfilled. Or was the difficulty more fundamental? Did the world expect two roles from one man, when experience should have clearly indicated that ability to play the two are seldom com bined in the same person? The power to make the statement, to idealize a given situation, to formulate the principle, is a gift of the highest sort, but it assumes with intellectual power a certain ability of philosophic detachment; in one sense it implies the spectator rather than the doer. A man who has thus formulated a situation must have a sense of achievement, of having done what he is best fitted to do; he has made his contribution and it is almost inevitable that he should feel that the thing itself has been accomplished. To require the same man later on to carry out his dictum in a complicated, contradictory situation demands such a strain upon his temperament that it may be expecting him to do what only another man of quite another temperament could do. Certainly international affairs have been profoundly modified by President Wilsons magnificent contribution. From one aspect of the situation he did obtain his end; to urge "open covenants, openly arrived at" as a basic necessity for a successful society of nations, cuts at the root of a prolific cause for war by simply turning on the light. But the man who would successfully insist upon such a course of procedure in actual negotiations is not only he who sees the situation but he who is bent upon the attainment of a beloved object, whose cause has become his hearts desire. Nothing can ever destroy the effect of the public utterance of the phrase, and the President may well contend that to have aided in the establishment of a League of Nations Secretariat where all treaties must be registered before they are valid is, in fact, the accomplishment of his dictum, although he must inevitably encounter the disappointment of those who believed it to imply an open discussion of the terms of the Peace Treaty, which to his mind was an impossibility. Such an interpretation may explain the paradox that the author of the fourteen points returned from Paris, claiming that he had achieved them.

Naturally, during the war, there was little that pacifist organizations could do; from time to time we put out suggestions, sending them directly to those government authorities who were responsible for the policies recommended. Our small group was much disturbed as were other American citizens, by what became increasingly obvious as the war progressed, that the policies of the war as well as its actual conduct were falling into the hands of the militarists.

We proposed at our fourth annual meeting that a beginning be made by the Allies to form an Executive Council not only for political action at the present but for the future as well. "We suggested that Great Britain, France and the U. S. A. each appoint three delegates to an Allied Political Council; that Italy and Japan each appoint two delegates; that the other nations associated in military opposition to Germany each appoint one delegate; that these delegates meet in London and organize in a deliberative and advisory capacity. We hoped that it could assume as much positive authority as the Versailles Military Council was at that moment exercising, not only in military matters but ultimately in civil affairs as well. Some such policy did later of course develop, through the Supreme Economic Council, although a travesty of what we had hoped for.

As pacifists were in a certain sense outlaws during the war, our group was no longer in direct communication with the White House, which was of course to be expected, although curiously enough we only slowly detached ourselves from the assumption that the President really shared our convictions. He himself at last left no room for doubt, when in November he declared before the American Federation of Labor that he had a contempt for pacifists because "I, too, want peace, but I know how to get it, and they do not." We quite agreed with him that he knew how if he meant to secure peace through a League of Nations, but we could not understand how he hoped to do it through war.

I heard President Wilson speak in New York in Carnegie Hall in February, 1919, just before he returned to Europe for the continuance of the Peace Conference, where he stressed the fact that the treaty and the League would be inextricably woven together. Later in the same speech, when he said "that those who oppose the League must be deaf to the demands of the common man the world over," I could not but speculate why, therefore, must the League depend upon the treaty? How far had it been his war experiences which had led him to place his trust in treaties, above his trust in the instincts of humble people, in whose hearts the desire for peace had at last taken sanctuary?

CHAPTER IV

A REVIEW OF BREAD RATIONS AND WOMANS TRADITIONS

As the European war continued and new relief organizations developed for the care of the wounded and orphaned, the members of our group felt increasingly the need for the anodyne of work, although it was difficult to find our places. For instance, the American Red Cross, following the practice of the British society, had become part of the military organization as it had never done before and its humanitarian appeal for funds had fully utilized the war enthusiasms. Such a combination made it not only more difficult for pacifists to become identified with the Red Cross, but all war activities which were dependent upon public funds became very timid in regard to pacifist cooperation. This was, of course, quite natural as the newspapers constantly coupled the words traitor and pro-German with the word pacifist, as if they described one and the same person. There were in fact many examples arising from the fear of imperiling a good cause by having a pacifist identified with it, that resulted in indi vidual pacifists withdrawing from organizations which they had themselves founded or fostered. But although our feelings were sometimes hurt at the moment when it was made obvious that one or another was persona non grata, I think, on the whole, we frankly recognized the instinct for practical politics as responsible for certain incidents; at any rate, we learned to take our rebuffs without a sense of grievance. Personally, I found these incidents easier to bear than the occasional persecutions which came the other way around; when enthusiastic and fanatical pacifists openly challenged the honesty and integrity of their former associates who had become convinced of the necessity for the war.

With many other Americans I, therefore, experienced a great sense of relief when Congress finally established a Department of Food Administration for the United States and when Mr. Hoover, who had spent two and a half years in Europe in intimate contact with the backwash of war, made his first appeal to his fellow countrymen in the name of the food shortage of the entire world, insisting that "the situation is more than war, it is a problem of humanity."

Certainly here was a line of activity into which we might throw ourselves with enthusiasm, and if we were not too conspicuous we might be permitted to work without challenge. The latter was perhaps too much to hope for. But although the challenge came from time to time, in my case at least it did not prove a deterrent and I was soon receiving many more invitations than I could possibly accept to speak on food conservation in relation to European needs; some of these invitations were under the auspices of the Federal Department of Food Administration, and in California, Texas, Colorado and other states under the auspices of the State. But what I cared most for was an opportunity to speak to womens organizations, because I not only believed, as I somewhat elaborately stated, that "in this great undertaking women may bear a valiant part if they but stretch their minds to comprehend what it means in this world crisis to produce food more abundantly and to conserve it with wisdom," but I also believed that we might thus break through into more primitive and compelling motives than those inducing so many women to increase the war spirit. There was something as primitive and real about feeding the helpless as there was about the fighting and in the race history the tribal feeding of children antedated mass fighting by perhaps a million years. Anthropologists insist that war has not been in the world for more than 20,000 years. It is in fact so recent that existing remnants of primitive people do not understand it. They may be given to individual murder but not to the col lective fighting of numbers of men against other masses of men. Could not the earlier instinct and training in connection with food be aroused and would it be strong enough to overwhelm and quench the later tendency to war. Each individual within himself represented something of both strains: I used to remind myself that although I had had ancestors who fought in all the American wars since 1684, I was also the daughter, granddaughter and the great granddaughter of millers. My earliest recollection was of being held up in a pair of dusty hands to see the heavy stone mill wheels go round. The happiest occupation of my childhood was to watch the old foaming water wheel turning in the back of the mill. I could tell by the sound of the mill when the old wheel was used, which occurred occasionally long after the turbines were established. Watching the foaming water my childish mind followed the masses of hard yellow wheat through the processes of grinding and bolting into the piled drifts of white flour and sometimes further into myriad bowls of bread and milk.

Again, those two strains of War and Bread mingled in my memory of months of travel. Certainly drilling soldiers and the constant reviewing of troops were seen in all the capital cities of Europe but there were also the peasant women who, all the world over, are still doing such a large part of the work connected with the growing and preparation of foods. I recalled them everywhere in the fields of vast Russia as in the tiny pastures of Switzerland; by every roadside in Palestine they were grinding at the hand mills; in Egypt they were forever carrying the water of the Nile that the growing corn might not perish.

The newspapers daily reported the changing fortunes of war on both fronts and our souls turned sick with anxiety and foreboding because all that the modern world held dear hung upon the hazards of battle. But certainly the labor for bread, which to me was more basic and legitimate than war, was still going on everywhere. In my desire to uncover it, to make clear womans traditional activity with something of its poetry and significance, I read endlessly in Erasers "Golden Bough," two large volumes of which are given over to the history and interpretation of the innumerable myths dealing with the Spirits of the Corn. These spirits are always feminine and are usually represented by a Corn Mother and her daughter, vaguely corresponding to the Greek Demeter–the always fostering Earth, and her child Persephone.

At the risk of breaking into the narrative of this book, so far as there is one, I am venturing to repeat some of the material which brought a touch of comfort to me and which, so far as I was able at that moment, I handed on to other women. Fraser discovers that relics of the Corn Mother and the Corn Maiden are found in nearly all the harvest fields of Europe; among many tribes of North American Indians; the Eastern world has its Rice Mother, for whom there are solemn ceremonies when the seed rice, believed to contain "soul stuff," is gathered. These deities are always feminine, as is perhaps natural from the association with fecundity and growth, and about them has gathered much of the poetry and song in the sowing of the grain and the gathering of the harvest, and those saddest plaints of all, expressing the sorrows of famine.

Myths centering about the Corn Mother but dimly foreshadowed what careful scientific researches have later verified and developed. Students of primitive society believe that women were the first agriculturists and were for a long time the only inventors and developers of its processes. The men of the tribe did little for cultivating the soil beyond clearing the space and sometimes surrounding it by a rough protection. The woman as consistently supplied all cereals and roots eaten by the tribe as the man brought in the game and fish, and in early picture writing the short hoe became as universally emblematic of woman as the spear of the hunter, or the shield and battle axe of the warrior. In some tribes it became a fixed belief that seeds would not grow if planted by a man, and apparently all primitive peoples were convinced that seeds would grow much better if planted by women. In Central Africa to this day a woman may obtain a divorce from her husband and return to her fathers tribe, if the former fails to provide her with a garden and a hoe.

It is said that every widespread myth has its counterpart in the world of morals. This is certainly true of the "fostering Mother." Students in the origin of social customs contend that the gradual change from the wasteful manner of nomadic life to a settled and much more economic mode of existence may be fairly attributed to these primitive agricultural women. Mothers in order to keep their children alive had transplanted roots from the forest or wild grains from the plains, into patches of rudely cultivated ground. We can easily imagine when the hunting was poor or when the flocks needed a new pasture, that the men of the tribe would be for moving on, but that the women might insist that they could not possibly go until their tiny crops were garnered; and that if the tribe were induced to remain in the same caves or huts until after harvest the women might even timidly hope that they could use the same fields next year, and thus avert the loss of their children, sure to result from the alternation of gorging when the hunt was good and of starv ing when it was poor. The desire to grow food for her children led to a fixed abode and to the beginning of a home, from which our domestic morality and customs are supposed to have originated.

With such a historic background, it seemed to me that women might, in response to the food saving and food production appeals issued in one country after another, so enlarge their conception of duty that the consciousness of the worlds needs for food should become the actual impulse of their daily activities.

It also presented another interesting aspect; from the time we were little children we have all of us, at moments at least, cherished overwhelming desires to be of use in the great world, to play a conscious part in its progress. The difficulty has always been in attaching our vague purposes to the routine of our daily living, in making a synthesis between our ambitions to cure the ills of the world on the one hand, and the need to conform to household requirements on the other.

It was a very significant part of the situation, therefore, that at this worlds crisis the two had become absolutely essential to each other. A great world purpose could not be achieved without womans participation founded upon an intelligent understanding and upon the widest sympathy, at the same time the demand could be met only if it were attached to her domestic routine, its very success depending upon a conscious change and modification of her daily habits.

It was no slight undertaking to make this synthesis, it afforded probably the most compelling challenge which has been made upon womans constructive powers for centuries. It required all her human affection and all her clarity of mind to make the kind of adjustment which the huge scale of the situation demanded.

It is quite understandable that there was no place for woman and her possible contribution in international affairs under the old diplomacy. Such things were indeed not "womans sphere." But it was possible that as women entered into politics when clean milk and the premature labor of children became factors in political life, so they might be concerned with international affairs when these at last were dealing with such human and poignant matters as food for starving peoples who could be fed only through international activities.

I recall a great audience in Hot Springs, Arkansas, made up of the members of the General Federation of Womens Clubs. It seemed to me that every woman there might influence her community "back home," not only to produce and to save more food, but to pour into the war torn world such compassion as would melt down its animosities and bring back into it a gregarious instinct older and more human that the motives responsible for war. I believed that a generous response to this world situation might afford an opportunity to lay over again the foundations for a wider, international morality, as womans concern for feeding her children had made the beginnings of an orderly domestic life. We are told that when the crops of grain and roots so painstakingly produced by primitive women began to have a commercial value their production and exchange were taken over by the men, as men later turned the manufacturing of pottery and other of womans early industries into profit making activities. Such a history, suggested that this situation might be womans opportunity if only because foods were, during the war, no longer considered primarily in regard to their money-making value but from the point of view of their human use. Because the production of food was, for the moment, dependent upon earlier motives, it had fallen back into womans hands. There had developed a wide concern for the feeding of hungry people, an activity with which women were normally connected.

As I had felt the young immigrant conscripts caught up into a great world movement, which sent them out to fight, so it seemed to me the millions of American women might be caught up into a great world purpose, that of conservation of life; there might be found an antidote to war in womans affection and all-embracing pity for helpless children.

Certainly compassion is not without its social utility. Up to the present moment the nations, in their foreign policies, have conspicuously lacked that humane quality which has come in their domestic policies through the increasing care for the poor, and the protection of children. These have been responsible for all sorts of ameliorative legislation during the later years, in one nation after another. In their relations to each other, however, nations have been without such motives of humanitarian action until the Allied nations, during the war, evolved a strikingly new foreign policy in their efforts to relieve the starvation and distress throughout widespread areas.

There are such unexpected turnings in the paths of moral evolution that it would not be without precedent that a new and powerful force might be unloosed in the world when the motive for producing and shipping food on the part of great nations was no longer a commercial one but had for the moment shifted to a desire to feed hungry people with whose governments they had entered into obligations. Such a force might in the future have to be reckoned with as a factor in international affairs.

In those dark years, so destructive of the old codes, the nations were forced back to their tribal function of producing and conserving food in contrast to the methods of modern commerce. All food supplies had long been collected and distributed through the utilization of the commercial motive. When it was commercially valuable to a man, to a firm or nation, food was shipped; when it was not commercially valuable, food was withheld or even destroyed. At that moment, however, the Allied Nations were collecting and conserving a common food supply and each nation was facing the necessity of making certain concessions to the common good that the threat of famine for all might be averted. A new internationalism was being established day by day; the making of a more reasonable world order, so cogently urged by the President of the United States, was to some extent already under way, the war itself forming its matrix.

There was a substitution of the social utility motive for that of commercial gain, energized pity for that of business enterprise. Mr. Hoover had said: "The wheat loaf has ascended in the imagination of enormous populations as the positive symbol of national survival.1 It seemed as if the age-long lack of organization between the nations, the dearth of human relationships in world politics, was about to be corrected, because an unspeakable disaster had forced the nations to consider together the primitive questions of famine and pestilence. It was possible that a new international ethic was arising from these humble beginnings, as the defense and feeding of the dependent members of the tribe had laid the foundations of tribal loyalty and of national existence itself. In spite of the great mass of social data accumulated in the last century, in spite of widespread intellectual training, there has been no successful attempt to reduce the chaos of human affairs into a rational world order. Society failed to make a community of nations and was at last tragically driven to the beginnings of one along the old primitive folkways, as if in six thousand years no other method could have been devised. It seemed, therefore, a great historic achievement that there should have been devised a workable method for the collective purchase of food, to prohibit profiteering in "the precious stuff that men live by," even for the duration of the war. We had all been much impressed by the methods of food distribution in Belgium. Fifteen million dollars each month were lent to that unhappy nation by the United States, which had taken over the responsibility of feeding her beleaguered population. This amount was spent in the United States for food and its value was carefully considered by the Division of Research in Nutritive Value in the Department of Food Administration. This Division undertook to know, as well as science could tell, what were the necessary daily rations to maintain health and strength in the several occupations, and how the requirements could best be met from the stores on hand. Such words as "adequate nutrition" and "physiological values" had been made practical issues and the administrative world represented by governmental officials was then seriously considering the production of food and the feeding of human beings in the light of pure science.

As a result, the political relations at least between Belgium and her Allies had completely shifted from the commercial to the humanitarian. To quote again from a speech of Mr. Hoovers: "For trree years three million bushels monthly of North American wheat, largely from the charity of the world, has been the daily bread of ten million human beings in Belgium and Northern France. To those who doled out this scant allowance, wheat became indelibly the precious symbol of life."

To transfer this concern for food into the international field was to enlarge its functions enormously as well as to increase its proportions. The Allied Nations had seriously undertaken to solve the problem of producing with the utmost economy of human labor the largest amount of food and of distributing that food to the points of greatest need, they had been forced to make international arrangements for its distribution, exactly as intelligently as they were producing war supplies.

It was easier to do this because each of the Allied Nations, in additions to feeding the soldiers and the munition makers who were directly concerned in the tragic business of "winning the war," had also become responsible for feeding its entire civilian population. The appointment of food controllers, the issuing of bread cards and the system of rationing, was undertaken quite as much in the interest of just dealing in food supplies as for food conservation itself. The British government, in the winter of 1916, when we were constantly speaking on food conservation as such, had undertaken the responsibility of providing the British Isles with all its imported food, and other belligerent and neutral nations had been obliged to pursue the same course in order to avert starvation. Commercial competition had been suppressed, not in response to any theory, but because it could not be trusted to Teed the feeble and helpless. The European governments had been compelled to undertake, as the consequence of the shortage in materials, the single-handed purchase of their supplies both for civil and military purposes. There had grown up an enormous consolidation of buying for a hundred and twenty million European people—a phenomenon never before witnessed in the economic history of the world.

With this accomplishment, it seemed reasonable to hope for world order in other directions as well. Certainly some of the obstructions were giving way. An English economist had said in 1917: "The war has, so far, in Europe generally, thrown the customs tariff flat." Were they, perhaps, disappearing under this onslaught of energized pity for world-wide needs, and was a motive power, new in the relations between nations being evolved in response to hunger and dependence as the earliest domestic ethics had been? It was becoming clear that nations cannot oppose their political frontiers as an obstacle to free labor and exchange without suffering themselves and causing suffering; that the world was faced with a choice between freedom in international commerce or international conflicts of increasing severity. Under this new standard of measurement, preferential tariffs would inevitably disappear because the nation denied the open door must suffer in its food supplies; the control of strategic waterways or interstate railroad lines by any one nation which might be tempted to consider only the interest of its own commerce, would become unthinkable. All that then would be necessary to secure the in ternationalization of the Straits of Bosphorus would be a demonstration of the need in Western Europe for Russian wheat, which had hitherto been exported so capriciously; the international building and control of a railroad into Mesopotamia would depend, not upon the ambition of rival nations, but upon the worlds need of the food which could again be secured from the capacious valley of the Euphrates by the restoration of the canal system so long ago destroyed. Serbia would be assured a railroad to the sea through a strip of international territory, because ready access to sea-going ships is so necessary to a nations food and because one of the principal causes of the economic friction that so often lies behind wars is the fear of countries that have no ports lest the neighboring country through which their export and import trade has to pass should hamper and interrupt the transit.

Certainly during the winter of 1916-17 I, personally, came to believe it possible that the more sophisticated questions of national grouping and territorial control would gradually adjust themselves if the paramount human question of food for the hungry were fearlessly and drastically treated upon an international basis. I ventured further, that the League of Nations, upon which the whole world, led by President Wilson, was fastening its hopes, might be founded not upon broken bits of international law, but upon ministrations to primitive human needs.

Much had been said during the war about primitive emotion and instinctive action, but certainly their use need not be reserved to purposes of destruction. After all, the first friendly communication between tribe and tribe came through the need of food when one or the other was starving and too weak to fight; primitive human compassion made the folkway which afterward developed into political relationships. I dared to believe that this early human instinct to come together in order to avert widespread starvation could not be forever thwarted by appeals to such later separatist instincts as nationalism and therefore urged that the gates be opened and that these primitive emotions be allowed to flood our devastated world. By all means let the beneficent tide be directed and canalized by the proposed League of Nations which was, after all, the outgrowth of century old dreams.

CHAPTER V.

A SPECULATION ON BREAD LABOR AND WAR SLOGANS.

It was at the end of the winter of 1916-17 that the astounding news came of the Russian Revolution. Perhaps it was because this peasant revolution reminded me of Bondereffs "Bread Labour," a sincere statement of the aspirations of the Russian peasants, that the events during the first weeks of the revolution seemed to afford a sharp contrast between the simple realities of life and the unreal slogans with which the war was being stimulated. Years of uncertainty, of conflicting reports, and of disillusionment, which have followed the Russian Revolution of March 1917, make it difficult to recall our first impressions of the most astounding phenomenon in this astounding world as the two thousand miles of Russian soldiers along the Eastern Front in the days following the abdication of the Czar talked endlessly to their enemy brothers in the opposing trenches.

During their long conversation the Russian peasant soldiers were telling the East Prussian peasant soldiers what Bondereff and other peasant leaders had told them: that the great task of this generation of Russians is to "free the land" as a former generation had already freed the serfs and slaves; that the future of the Russian peasant depends not upon garrisons and tax gatherers but upon his willingness to perform "bread labor" on his recovered soil, and upon his ability to extend good will and just dealing to all men. With their natural inference that there was no longer any need to carry on the Czars war was an overwhelming eagerness to get back to the land which they believed was at last to be given those who actually tilled it. They doubtless said that the peasants had long been holding themselves in readiness for the great revolution which would set men free from brutal oppression. They believed that this revolution must, before all, repair "the great crime," which in their minds was always the monopolization of the land by a few thousand men with the resulting enslavement of millions of others. The revolution must begin in Russia because no people are so conscious of this iniquity as the Russian people. Their absorption in the revolution and their inveterate land hunger caused many Russian peasants to regard the world war itself as a mere interruption to the fulfillment of their supreme obligation.

It was certainly the wisdom of the humble, the very counsel of imperfection, which was exemplified by this army of tattered men, walking so naively in the dawning light. But they may have been "the unhindered and adventuring sons of God," as they renounced warfare in favor of their old right to labor in the ground. Some of them in the earliest days of the revolution made a pilgrimage to Tolstoys grave in the forest of Kadaz and wrote these words upon a piece of paper which they buried in the leaf mold lying loosely above him: "Love to neighbors, nay the greatest love of all, love to enemies, is now being accomplished." In the Russian peasants dread of war there has always been a passive resistance to the reduction of the food supply, because he well knows that when a man is fighting he ceases to produce food and that the world will at length be in danger of starvation. Next to the masses of India and China, the Russian peasants feel the pinch of hunger more frequently than any other people on earth. Russia is the land of modern famines; the present one was preceded by those of 1891, 1906, and 1911. The last, still vivid in the memory of men at the front, affected thirty million people, and reduced eight million people to actual starvation. The Russian peasant saw three and a half years of the Great War, during which time, according to his own accounting, seven million of his people perished and the Russian soldiers, never adequately equipped with ammunition, food and clothing, were reduced to the last extremity. To go back to his village, to claim his share of food, to till the ground as quickly as possible, was to follow an imperative and unerring instinct. In his village, if anywhere, he would find bread. Prince Kropotkin in his "Conquest of Bread"–written nearly twenty years ago–predicted that so soon as The Revolution came, the peasant would keep enough bread for himself and his children, but that the towns and cities would experience such a dearth of grain that "the farmers in America could hardly be able to cover it." But he adds: "There will be an increase of production as soon as the peasant realizes that he is no longer forced to support the idle rich by his toil. New tracts of land will be cleared and improved machines set agoing. Never was the land so energetically cultivated as by the French peasants in 1792."

In line with these peasant traditions, the first appeal issued by the All Russian Peasant Union to the soldier still at the front read in this wise:

"Remember, brothers that the Russian army is a peasant army, comprising now the best men of the whole peasantry; that the Russian land is the peasants land; that the peasant is the principal toiler on this land–he is its master, therefore, without the master it is impossible to solve properly the land question."

Peasants all over the world magnify and consider obligatory labor in the ground, but the Russian peasant adds to this urge for bread labor a religious motive revealed in his formal greeting to his fellow-workman in the field: "To every man his measure of grain, and may every man in the world be a Christian." This mystic connection between piety and bread labor has, of course, been expressed in many forms; to quote from an English poet:

"And when I drove the clods apart
Christ would be plowing in my heart."

Or from a French one:

"Au milieu du grand silence, le pays
se recusille soucieusement, tandis que, pas
a pas, priante, la Lucie laisse, un a un,
tomber les grains qui luisent."

Or from a Norwegian:

"The sower walked bare-headed in Jesus name. Every cast was made with care in a spirit of kindly resignation; so it is throughout all the world where corn is sown. little showers of grain flung at famine from the sowers hand,"

Certainly tilling the soil, living a life of mutual labor has been at the bottom of many religious orders and mystic social experiments. From this point of view, Tolstoy had rejoiced that groups of Russian peasants had never owned land but had worked it always with the needs of the whole village in mind, thus keeping close to Christian teaching and to a life of piety.

That this instinct of bread labor, the very antithesis of war, is wide-spread may be easily demonstrated. A newspaper clipping on my desk contains a dispatch from Bressa in Asia Minor, which reads as follows: "The country had been revived by rains with the awakening of spring, and peasants are seen working in the fields, kissing the earth and thanking Allah for the blessed rain and also praying for peace and the riddance from the lands of the soldiers marching across to war."

When we were in Austria-Hungary in 1915, we were constantly told stories of Russian soldiers who throughout the spring had easily been taken prisoners because they had heard that war prisoners in Austria were working upon the land. These Russian peasant soldiers had said to their captors, now that spring had come they wanted to get back to work, and so they would like to be made prisoners at least long enough to put the seed into the ground. They wished to put seed into the ground irrespective of its national or individual ownership.

I recall an evening years ago when I sat in the garden at Yasnaya Polyana, that Tolstoy begged us to remember that the Russian peasant did not change his nature when he shed his blouse and put on the Czars coat. Tolstoy predicted that the Russian peasants in their permanent patience, their insatiable hunger for bread labor, may at last make war impossible to an entire agricultural people. It is hard to determine whether the Russian soldiers who, in 1917, refused to fight, had merely become so discouraged by their three years of futile warfare and so cheered by the success of a bloodless revolution in Petrograd and Moscow that they dared to venture the same tactics in the very trenches, or whether these fighting men in Galicia yielded to an instinct to labor on the land which is more primitive and more imperative than the desire for war.

During the early days of the Russian revolution it seemed to me that events bore out the assumption that the Russian peasants, with every aspect of failure, were applying the touchstone of reality to certain slogans evolved during the war, to unreal phrases which had apparently gripped the leading minds of the world. It was in fact the very desire on the part of the first revolutionists in the spring of 1917 to stand aside from political as well as from military organizations and to cling only to what they considered the tangible realities of existence, which was most diffi cult for the outside world to understand. The speculation as I recall it, evolved in my mind somewhat as follows:

The many Allied nations in the midst of a desperate war, were being held together by certain formulae of their war aims which had gradually emerged during long years of mutual effort. Such stirring formulae or statements could be common to all the diverse Allies, however, only if they took on the abstract characteristics of general principles. This use of the abstract statement, necessary in all political relationships, becomes greatly intensified in time of war, as if illustrating the contention that men die willingly only for a slogan. The question inevitably suggested itself: Had the slogans–this is a war to end war and a war to safeguard the world for democracy–become so necessary to united military action that the Allies resented the naive attempt on the part of the Russian peasants to achieve democracy without war? They so firmly believed that the aims of the war could only be accomplished through a victory of the Allies that they would not brook this separation of the aim from the method. Apparently the fighting had become an integral part of the slogan itself.

The necessity for holding fast to such phrases suggests one of those great historic myths which large bodies of men are prone to make for them selves when they unite in a common purpose requiring for its consummation the thorough and efficient output of moral energy. Mankind is so fertile in virtue and heroism, so prone to transcend his own powers, that the making and unmaking of these myths always accompanies a period of great moral awakening. Such myths are almost certain to outlast their social utility, and very often they outlive their originators; as the myth of The Second Coming evolved by the Early Christians held for a thousand years.

Had this myth of our contemporaries that Democracy is to be secured through war, so obsessed the Allies that they were constrained to insist that the troops fight it out on the eastern front as elsewhere, in spite of the fact that fraternal intercourse, which the Russians were employing, is the very matrix of Democracy? Had war so militarized and clericalized the leading nations of the world that it was difficult for them to believe that the Russian soldiers, having experienced that purification of the imagination and of the intellect which the Greeks believed to come through pity and terror, had merely been the first to challenge the myth, to envisage the situation afresh and reduce it to its human terms 1

Vernon Lee contends that it is the essential characteristic of an historic myth that so long as it does not attempt to produce its own realization, it begets unhesitating belief and wholesale action and that as men go on expressing it with sufficient self-denying fervor, they secure a great output of sanctity and heroism. The necessity for continuing this output, of unifying diverse nations, may account for the touch of fear easily detected on the part of the ardent advocates of war, when they were asked not to ignore the fact that at least on one front war was actually ending under conditions of disarmament and free trade. They did not admit that democracy could be established throughout one-sixth of the earths surface only if the Allies would recognize the fact that the Russian soldiers had ceased to fight; Kerenskys group, or any other remaining in power, would at length have been obliged to acknowledge it for no governmental group could have been upheld by the Russian people unless it had declared for peace and for free land.

Did the Allies fear to jar the abstraction which had become so dear to them? Did they realize instinctively that they would cripple the usefulness of a slogan by acknowledging its partial achievement?

It was perhaps to be expected that Russia should be the first nation to apply the touchstone of reality to a warring world so absorbed in abstractions. If Tolstoy may be considered in any sense the prototype of his countrymen, it may be permitted to cite his inveterate dislike of abstractions, whether stated in philosophic, patriotic or religious terms; his firm belief that such abstractions lay the foundation for blind fanaticism; his oft-repeated statement that certain forms of patriotism are inimical to a life of reason.

At that time the Allied nations were all learning to say that the end of this war would doubtless see profound political changes and democratic reconstruction, when the animalistic forces which are inevitably encouraged as a valuable asset in warfare, should once more be relegated to a subordinate place. And yet when one of the greatest possible reconstructions was actually happening before their very eyes, the war-weary world insisted that the Russian soldier should not be permitted to return to the land but should continue to fight. This refusal on the part of the Allied Governments suggests that they were so obsessed by the dogmatic morality of war, in which all humanly tangible distinctions between normal and abnormal disappear, that they were literally blind to the moral implications of the Russian attempt.

The Russian soldiers, suddenly turned into propagandists, inevitably exhibited a youthful self-consciousness which made their own emotional experience the center of the universe. Assuming that others could not be indifferent to their high aims, they placidly insisted upon expounding their new-found hopes. But all this made the warring world, threatened with defeat if the German army on the eastern front were released, still more impatient.

Possibly, as a foolish pacifist, wishing to see what was not there, I gave myself over to idle speculation. It may be true that the spiritual realism as well as the real politik was with the Allied statesmen who forced Kerensky to keep his men at war even at the price of throwing Russia into dire confusion.

These statesmen considered the outcome of the Russian Revolution of little moment compared to the future of civilization which was then imperilled by the possibility of a German victory if the men on the eastern front were allowed to reinforce the west. But such an assumption based on the very doctrines of war, was responsible for Brest Litovsk; for "peace after a smashing victory;" for the remarkable terms in the Versailles treaty; for Trotskys huge army; for much of the present confusion in the world. Did the Russians, for one golden moment, offer a way out? or was the present outcome inevitable?

Three times in crucial moments in the worlds history and with a simple dramatic gesture have representatives of Russia attempted to initiate the machinery which should secure permanent peace for all nations.

First: the proposals of the Russian Czar, Alexander I, in 1815, at the Peace Conference following the Napoleonic Wars, for "An All-Embracing Reform of the political system of Europe which should guarantee universal peace" and the resulting Holy Alliance which, according to historians, did not succeed "owing to the extremely religious character in which it was conceived."

Second: the calling of the first Hague Conference by Nicholas II, in 1899. His broad outline of the work which such a conference ought to do was considered "too idealistic" by the other powers, who tried to limit the function of the Hague Conferences to the reduction of armaments and to the control of the methods of warfare.

Third: the spontaneous effort of the first Russian revolutionists to break through the belief that any spiritual good can be established through the agency of large masses of men fighting other large masses and their naive attempt to convert individual soldiers. The string of Russian soldiers talking to their recent enemies stretched from the Baltic sea to the Carpathian Mountains. These simple men assumed that men wished to labor in the soil and did not wish to fight, while all the rest of the world remained sceptical and almost rejoiced over the failure of the experiment, before it had really been tried. Certainly the world was in no mood just then to listen to "mere talk." It was resounding with a call to arms.

With our Anglo-Saxon crispness of expression we are prone to be amused at the Russians inveterate habit of discussion and to quote with tolerant contempt the old saying: "Two Russians–three opinions," without stopping to reflect that the method has in practice worked out excellently for the self-governing administration of village affairs throughout an enormous territory.

When the first detachment of Russian Doukho-boritsi were settling in Western Canada, they discussed for two and a half days and two nights the location of the three villages into which the detachment was divided. One possible site was very much more desirable than the other two and the Anglo-Saxon onlooker feared that this factor alone might indefinitely prolong the difficulty of decision. But not at all–the discussion came to a natural end, the matter was settled and never again reopened nor was the disparity and the desirability of the locations ever again referred to by anyone concerned. The matter had been satisfactorily settled in the prolonged discussion by all the "souls" entitled to participate. It proved after all to have been a very good way.

We forget that to obtain the "inner consent" of a man who differs from us is always a slow process, that quite as it is quicker to punish an un ruly child than to bring him to a reasonable state of mind; to imprison a criminal than to reform him; to coerce an ignorant man than to teach him the meaning of the law, so it is quicker to fight armies of men than to convince them one by one.

A curious and very spontaneous manifestation of good-will towards Russia occurred in Chicago in the spring of 1918. A society was organized with the slogan: "Ten Million Pairs of Shoes for Russia," and ten thousand old shoes were actually collected and placed in a warehouse. The pro-motors contended that all of the Russian peasants knew how to work in leather and could make their own shoes if they but had the material with which to work. In response to the objection that even if it were practicable to send the shoes they might easily fall into the hands of the Germans, the reply was always the same; that although there might be a risk of Germanys seizing the goods sent into Russia, if the United States did nothing at all in Russias period of greatest distress and need, we ran the risk that Germany would obtain the goodwill of all Russia and that America would suffer an alienation and misunderstanding from which we might never recover. Of course, Anglo-Saxon good sense prevailed in the end and the collected shoes were never sent, although there is no doubt that even such a homely expression of good-will would have been most valuable for the future relations between the two countries. Throughout the discussion I sometimes remembered what a famous British statesman wrote to Charles Sum-ner in 1862 concerning the cotton spinners of Lancashire who were starving owing to the withdrawal of Southern cotton, but who nevertheless held to their principle that slave-grown cotton was an infamy: "Our people will be kept alive by the contributions of this country but I see that someone in the States had proposed to send something to our aid. If a few cargoes of flour could come, say 50,000 barrels, as a gift from persons in your northern states to the Lancashire workmen, it would have a prodigious effect in your favor here."

No one will be able to say how much it might have affected the sentiment toward the United States if such a humble cargo of good will had early left our shores for Russia, how it might have become the harbinger of other cargoes so long delayed 1

CHAPTER VI.

AFTER WAR WAS DECLARED.

The first meeting of our national Board, convened after the declaration of war, was in October, 1917, in a beautiful country house at which the members, arriving from New York, Boston, Philadelphia, St. Louis and Chicago, appeared as the guests at a house party, none of the friends of the hostess ever knowing that we had not been invited upon a purely social basis.

It was a blessed relief to be in communication with likeminded people once more and to lose somewhat the sense of social disapprobation and of alienation of which we had become increasingly conscious. After three days deliberation the Board issued a special manifesto to the various branches, beginning with the statement:

"All the activities of the Womans Peace Party have been, of course, modified by the entrance of the United States into the World War.

"We have avoided all criticism of our Government as to the declaration of war, and all activities that could be considered as obstructive in respect to the conduct of the war, and this not as a counsel of prudence, but as a matter of principle."

Because we saw even then that there was an element of hope in the international administration of food supplies and of other raw materials and clutched at it with something of the traditional desperation of the drowning man, the manifesto ended as follows:

"We recognize that an alliance between seventeen nations in both hemispheres cannot be confined to military operations. We rejoice in the fact that the United States of America has already taken common action with the Allies in regard to the conservation and distribution of food supplies and other matters, quite outside the military field, which require international cooperation. We venture to hope that conferences of this type may be extended until they develop into an international organization sitting throughout the war.

"An interparliamentary conference thus developed might from the nucleus of a per-manent international parliament eventually open to all nations. Such an organization of a World Parliament, arising in response to actual world needs, is in line with the genesis and growth of all permanent political institutions."

We could not then realize how very difficult it would be to make our position clear, and not for a long time did we sense the control of public opin ion and of all propaganda, which is considered necessary for the successful inauguration and conduct of war. What we were perhaps totally unprepared for as the war continued was the general unwillingness to admit any defect in the institution of war as such, or to acknowledge that, although exhibiting some of the noblest qualities of the human spirit, it yet affords no solution for vexed international problems; further we believed that after war has been resorted to, its very existence, in spite of its superb heroisms and sacrifices which we also greatly admired, tends to obscure and confuse those faculties which might otherwise find a solution. There was not only a reluctance to discuss the very issues for which the war was being fought, but it was considered unpatriotic to talk about them until the war had been won.

Even in the third month of the war, when asked to give an address before the City Club of Chicago on "Patriotism and Pacifists in War Time," I tried quite guilelessly to show that while the position of the pacifist in time of war is most difficult, nevertheless, the modern peace movement, since it was inaugurated three hundred years ago, had been kept alive throughout many great wars, and that even during the present one some sort of peace organization had been maintained in all of the belligerent nations. Our own Womans International Committee for Permanent Peace had organized branches since the war began in such fighting nations and colonies as Australia, Austria, Belgium, Canada, Finland, Germany, Great Britain, Ireland, Hungary, British India, Italy, France, Poland and Russia. I ventured to hope the United States would be as tolerant to pacifists in time of war as those countries had been, some of which were fighting for their very existence, and that our fellow-citizens, however divided in opinion, would be able to discuss those aspects of patriotism which endure through all vicissitudes.

It is easy enough now to smile at its naivete, but even then we were dimly conscious that in the stir of the heroic moment when a nation enters war, when mens minds almost without volition are driven back to the earliest obligations of patriotism, the emotions move along the worn grooves of blind admiration for the soldier and of unspeakable contempt for him who, in the hour of danger, declares that fighting is unnecessary. We were not surprised, therefore, when apparently striking across and reversing this popular conception of patriotism, we should be called traitors and cowards, but it seemed to us all the more necessary to demonstrate that in our former advocacy we were urging a reasonable and vital alternative to war. Only slowly did the pacifist realize that when his fellow countrymen are caught up by a wave of tremendous enthusiasm and are car ried out into a high sea of patriotic feeling the very virtues which the pacifist extols are brought into unhappy contrast to those which war, with its keen sense of a separate national existence, places in the foreground.

Yet in spite of this sober reasoning it was a distinct shock to me to learn that it had been difficult to secure a chairman to preside over the City Club meeting at which I spoke, and that even my old friends were afraid that the performance of this simple office would commit them to my pacifist position. I later lectured on the same subject at the University of Chicago, trying to be as "sweetly reasonable" as possible, but only to come out of the hall profoundly discouraged, having learned the lesson that during war it is impossible for the pacifist to obtain an open hearing. Nevertheless, we continued to talk, not from a desire of self-defense or justification, I think, for we had long since abandoned any such hope, but because we longed actually to modify the headlong course of events.

In the general mass of misunderstanding and deliberate misrepresentation some things were harder to bear than others. We were constantly accused of wishing to isolate the United States and to keep our country out of world politics. We were, of course, urging a policy exactly the reverse, that this country should lead the nations of the world into a wider life of co-ordinated political activity; that the United States should boldly recognize the fact that the vital political problems of our time have become as intrinsically international in character as have the commercial and social problems so closely connected with them. It seemed to us that the United States had to her credit a long account for the spread of democratic institutions during the years when she was at peace with the rest of the world. Her own experiment as a republic was quickly followed by France, and later by Switzerland, and to the south of her a vast continent contains no nation which fails, through many vicissitudes, to maintain a republican form of government. We also hoped to make clear that it has long been the aim of our own government and of similar types throughout the world to replace coercion by the full consent of the governed, to educate and strengthen the free will of the people through the use of democratic institutions; that this age-long process of obtaining the inner consent of the citizen to the outward acts of his government is of necessity violently interrupted and thrown back in war time.

Then some of us had once dreamed that the cosmopolitan inhabitants of this great nation might at last become united in a vast common endeavor for social ends. We hoped that this fusing might be accomplished without the sense of opposition to a common enemy which is an old method of welding people together, better fitted for military than for social use, adapted to a government resulting from coercion rather than one founded by free men.

We had also hoped much from the varied population of the United States; for whether we will or not, our very composition would make it easier for us than for any other nation to establish an international organization founded upon understanding and good will, did we but possess the requisite courage and intelligence to utilize it. There were in this country thousands of emigrants from Central Europe, to whom a war between the United States and the fatherland meant exquisite torture. They and their inheritances were a part of the situation which faced the United States in the spring of 1917; they were a source of great strength in an international venture, as they were undoubtedly a source of weakness in a purely nationalistic position of the old-fashioned sort. These ties of blood, binding us to all the nations of the earth, afforded, it seemed to us, a unique equipment for a great international task if the United States could but push forward into the difficult area of internationalism. Then too, the great war had already demonstrated that modern warfare is an intimately social and domestic affair. The civilian suffering and, in certain regions, the civilian mortality, were as great as that endured by the soldiers. There were thousands of our fellow citizens who could not tear their minds away from Poland, Galicia, Syria, Armenia, Serbia, Roumania, Greece, where their own relatives were dying from diseases superinduced by hardship and hunger. To such sore and troubled minds war had come to be a horror which belonged to Europe alone, and was part of that privation and oppression which they had left behind them when they came to America. Newly immigrated Austrian subjects of a dozen nationalities came to their American friends during the weeks of suspense before war was declared, utterly bewildered by the prospect of war. They had heard not three months before that the President of the United States did not believe in war–for so the campaign had been interpreted by many simple minds–and they had concluded that whatever happened, some more American way would be found. Pacifists hoped that this revolution in international relationships which had been steadily approaching for three hundred years and was already long over-due, could best be obtained after the war, if the United States succeeded in protecting and preserving the higher standards of internationalism. We were not unmindful of the hope for an international organization to be formed at the end of the war. But it seemed to us that for thirty three months Europe had been earnestly striving to obtain through patriotic wars, that which could finally be secured only through international organization. Millions of men, loyal to one international alliance, were gallantly fighting millions of men loyal to another international alliance, because of Europes inability to make an alliance including them all.

We also realized that ever since the European war began, the United States had been conscious of a failure to respond to a moral demand; she had vaguely felt that she was shirking her share in a world effort toward the higher good; she had had black moments of compunction and shame for her own immunity and safety. Could she hope through war to assuage the feverish thirst for action she had felt during all those three years? There is no doubt that she made the correct diagnosis of her case, of her weariness with a selfish, materialistic life and of her need for concerted, self-forgetting action. But was blood-letting a sufficiently modern remedy for such a diagnosis? Would she lose her sense of futility and her consciousness of moral failure, when thousands of her young men were facing the dangers of war? Would she not still feel her inadequacy unless she was able to embody in a permanent organization the cosmopolitanism which is the essence of her spirit? We feared she would not be content when she was obliged to organize food supplies solely for one group of nations, for the United States owed too much to all the nations of the earth whose sons had developed her raw prairies into fertile fields, to allow the women and children of any of them to starve.

At that moment the final outcome of the war was apparently to be decided quite as much by food supply as by force of arms. Two terrible questions were in mens minds. Could Germany hold out during the spring and early summer until the new crop was garnered? Could England feed herself were the U-boat campaign in any degree successful? For decades civilized nations had confidently depended upon other nations for their supply of cattle and of grain until this long continued war had brought the primitive fear of starvation back into the world with so many other elemental terrors.

Again and again we came back for comfort to the fact that the creation of an international organization of the Allies and Associated Powers for the control of their common food supply, was clearly transcending old national bounds. It might be a new phase of political unification in advance of all former achievements, or it might be one of those shifting alliances merely for war purposes, of which European history affords so many examples.

After war was declared, events moved with surprising rapidity. We had scarcely returned from Washington where we had been advocating a referendum on the declaration of war before we were back there again, this time protesting before the Military Affairs Committee that the measure of conscription should not be passed without an appeal to the country, without an expression of opinion from the simple people who form the rank and file of the soldiery in every war.

The most poignant moment during the war and the preparations for it, so far as I personally was concerned, came upon me suddenly one morning after a wretched night of internal debate. For many years one of the large rooms at Hull-House had been used for a polling place of the precinct, one election after another had been held there for some of which, after the women of Illinois had secured a large measure of the franchise, I had served as a judge of election. The room that morning was being used to register the men for the first draft. In they came somewhat heavily, one man after another, most of them South Italians. I knew many of them had come to this country seeking freedom from military service quite as much as they sought freedom of other sorts, and here they were about to be securely caught once more. The line of dull workmen seemed to me to represent the final frontier of the hopes of their kind, the traditional belief in America as a refuge had come to an end and there was no spot on the surface of the earth to which they might flee for security. All that had been told them of the American freedom, which they had hoped to secure for themselves and their children, had turned to ashes. I said nothing beyond the mornings greeting, but one of the men stopped to speak to me. He had been in the Hull-House citizenship classes, and only a few months before I had delivered a little address to those of the class who had received their first papers, combining congratulations with a welcome into the citizenship of the United States. The new citizen turned to me and spoke from the bitterness of his heart: "I really have you to thank if I am sent over to Europe to fight. I went into the citizenship class in the first place because you asked me to. If I hadnt my papers now I would be exempted." I could only reply that none of us knew what was going to happen and added, for what comfort it might give him, that at any rate he would be fighting on the side of Italy. But the incident did not add to my peace of mind.

Partly because one of the residents of Hull-House served as secretary to the local Draft Board, partly because the men were accustomed to come to the settlement for help of various kinds, we assisted many hundreds of them to fill out their questionnaires. The docility of the men was surprising; they were only too familiar with the whole process and had long ago accepted it as a part of life. The women sometimes begged us not to put down the ages of the little boys lest it might make it easier later for the government to conscript them, and they sometimes added: "They did this way over there, but we did not think it would be this way over here." When we served luncheons at Hull-House to the young men about to entrain for camp, the women folk were not admitted but hung in great crowds about the door, men and women alike entangled in a great world process of which they had no conception; it seemed to me at moments as if the whole theory of self-government founded upon conscious participation and inner consent, had fallen to the ground.

Later there were many cases of the immigrant bewildered and angered by the tax upon his former wages–an ex post facto arrangement which was equally trying to the employer and the immigrant, and proved so unworkable that it finally had to be abandoned. It was, however, a visible sign to the immigrant that he was suspect and undesirable, although he had come to the country in good faith and sincerely loved

America, but loved it perhaps as Lincoln once said of Henry Clay, "partly because it was his own and partly because it was a free country."

It is impossible to live for years among immigrants and to fail to catch something of their deep-seated hopes for the country of their adoption, to realize that the thought of America has afforded a moral safety valve to generations of oppressed Europeans. War and its conscriptions were something which belonged to the unhappy Europe they had left behind. It was as if their last throw had been lost. Of the 450,000,000 people in Europe 400,000,000 were already involved in the war. Could the United States do nothing more intelligent than to add its quota of 100,000,000 people more?

When it became evident that the measure for conscription would pass, those of us who had known something of the so-called conscientious objector in England hoped that we might at least obtain similar provisions for him in the United States. Although the English tribunals had power to grant absolute exemption from military service, there were in England at that time approximately six thousand men imprisoned or interned in addition to the number who were performing non-military service on the continent in such organizations as the Friends Ambulance Units.

A committee of us waited upon the Secretary of War, begging him to recommend like provision in the conscription measure then under consideration. The Secretary was ready to talk to our committee, each member of which could claim either acquaintance or friendship with him in the years before the war. He seemed so sympathetic and understanding that possibly we made too much of his somewhat cryptic utterance that "there would be no conscientious objector problem in the United States," and we left his office more reassured perhaps than we had any right to be.

It became evident in a very few weeks that no provision of any sort was to be made for the conscientious objector as such. Each man who objected to war could choose his own method of making his protest and be punished accordingly. If he failed to report for his assigned camp he was tried as a "deserter," if he refused to put on the uniform, the charge was insubordination; if he declined to drill or to obey an order, he might be court-martialed under the charge of resisting an officer, with a wide range of penalties, including imprisonment at Fort Leavenworth. Thus each camp had opportunity to treat the conscientious objector according to its own standard, but above all he was to be given no opportunity to make a dignified statement of his own case, no chance "to play the martyr or to hang out the white flag."

I saw the Secretary of War twice again on the matter, once with a committee and once alone, but it was evident that he had taken the same stand later formulated by the Administration in regard to other political prisoners, that there could be no such thing as a political offense in a democracy; each man was arrested for breaking a law and tried as a criminal. Any other course might have laid the government open to the charge of suppressing a minority, which was to be avoided. The reformer in politics knew only too well how to deal with the reformer out of politics. The latter was hoist by his own petard.

Only after hundreds of men had been placed in military prisons and separated in military camps under charge of violation of various sections of the military code, was a board appointed to review their cases, beginning work in June, 1919. This federal board endeavored to undo some of the injustices of the camps and to work out a system which, however vulnerable, was removed from the whim of individuals.

The word conscientious objector did not exactly apply to many of these young men whom I came to know, it is too rigid and too individualistic. Many of them felt that war was archaic and they were enveloped in a profound scepticism as to the possibility of securing democracy for the world through destruction of other young men possibly holding the same ideals for the future which they themselves cherished. They believed that any international league would have the best chance of success if it were started when the currents of brotherhood were flowing more strongly between the nations than is possible immediately after war.

In various ways I met many of them. I always urged each one if possible to conform to the military regulations. When a man himself decided that it was impossible I invariably heard his decision with a sinking of the heart. I recall a man who was one of three to object to war out of five thousand students in his college. He was segregated in an eastern camp and afterwards allowed to work under the Friends Service Committee in France, but finding that even non-combatant service did not bring him relief, returned from abroad preferring imprisonment to what seemed to him a dodging of the issue. Another had worked among war prisoners for nine months under the auspices of the Y. M. C. A. He found that he was being suspected of pacifism and was constantly watched and challenged by what amounted to a secret service system within the organization itself; it was a great relief for him to come home and "face the music," as he put it.

The sort of appeal to which he and his high minded kind were most persistently subjected could but recall the remark attributed to the emperor Diocletian as he saw the lions in the arena rip the throat of a young Christian: "that youth refused the military oath because his superstition commanded its followers not to bind themselves by swearing not to resist evil. These pitiful wretches enjoy the peace and splendor of Rome but will not move a finger to protect or to extend either." In all the centuries since, the state had found no better argument with which to coerce its minority who disapproved through religious scruple. But the early Christian could at least frankly call himself a martyr, and although he did not know that his blood would become the seed of the Church, he did know that he was bearing testimony to a new religion destined in time to supersede that of Diocletian; and the emperor himself, if he derided the new religion, at the same time more or less accurately defined it. Such satisfaction as that knowledge might have given to the young Christians of Rome was persistently denied the conscientious objector in the United States, and thousands of our fellow citizens to this day quite honestly confuse them with slackers.

Their history as inmates of federal prisons is being written and may yet inaugurate a chapter in prison reform, as the strike so successfully led by them in Leavenworth resulted in a brief trial of self-government for the entire prison. The tests in psychiatry showed that the average mentality of the conscientioius objector had registered well above that of the drafted men throughout the country in spite of the fact that many of their number had inherited their objections to war from teachings of simple religious sects and had never individually thought out their positions. Perhaps these latter at moments tasted martyrdom, but the more sophisticated men would have none of it.

Even the man tied by his wrists to the barred door of his cell for eight hours a day endeavored to keep free from self-pity. In a letter written to me from Leavenworth prison I find this statement:

"We do not think we are martyrs any more than a soldier taken prisoner by the enemy is a martyr."

Because years before I had been somewhat identified with the immigration of the Doukho-bortsi, a non-resistant Russian sect in whom Tolstoy had been much interested, I found myself appealed to on behalf of a frightened little widow who was at the moment desperately holding at bay the entire military prison system. Her husband had been one of "those obstinate cases who cling to a scriptural text and will not listen to reason." During his long imprisonments he had been treated in all sorts of barbarous ways and finally, after a prolonged ducking under a faucet in the prison yard on a freezing day, had contracted pneumonia and died. He had originally and continuously taken his stand against putting on the uniform, and when his wife arrived at Leaven-worth to take away the body, to her horror she found that body, at last unable to resist, dressed in a soldiers uniform. Her representative who came to see me, with his broken English, could convey but feebly the sense of outrage, of unfairness, of brutal disregard of the things of the spirit, of the ruthless overriding of personality which this incident had aroused among thousands of Doukhobortsi.

In camp and even in prison the conscientious objectors were constantly subjected to tremendous pressure by the chaplains to induce them to change their position, although in a sense they were denied the comforts of religion. Certainly the rest of us were. I recall going to church one beautiful summers day in 1917 when the family whom I was visiting urged me to hear a well known Bishop preach in the village church. The familiar words of the service could not be changed but the bishop was belligerent from his very first utterance and his peroration ended with the statement that if "Jesus were living to-day he would be fighting in the trenches of France." Not a word of the anxious, pitying, all-embracing love for lack of which the world was perishing I It was inevitable under these circumstances that new religious organizations should develop. The Fellowship of Reconciliation had, during 1915, attracted to its membership in Chicago a score of people, a few clergymen, one or two publicists and others who felt the need of meeting with like-minded people, and at least comparing their scruples and religious difficulties. We usually met in private houses on a social basis, as it were, not so much because we felt that a meeting discussing the teachings of Jesus could be considered "seditious," but from a desire to protect from publicity and unfriendly discussion the last refuge that was left us. We did not succeed even in that, although the unfair and hostile publicity came in a very curious way through the office of the Womans Peace Party, which one would suppose to be more open to attack than the Fellowship. Throughout the war the national office of the Womans Peace Party was kept open in a downtown office building in Chicago. We did not remove any of our records, being conscious that we had nothing to hide, and our list of members with their addresses was to be found in a conspicuous card catalogue case. It was often far from pleasant to enter the office. If a bit of mail protruded from the door it was frequently spat upon, and although we rented our quarters in a first class office building on Michigan boulevard facing the lake, the door was often befouled in hideous ways.

The secret service men finally entered the office in search of material not directly against us, but against the Fellowship of Reconciliation, which they considered as designed to lessen the morale of war. I have just read over some of the newspaper clippings; it is easy now to smile at their absurd efforts to give a sinister meaning to two such innocuous words as Fellowship and Reconciliation, but at the moment we all knew that it meant one more group put upon the index, as it were, and one more successful attempt to discredit pacifists. The only defense which in the least appealed to the newspaper men was made by one of themselves to the effect that the word reconciliation was very like in sound and purport to the word conciliation and that Nicholas Murray Butler was chairman of an organization to promote international arbitration and conciliation, and that every one knew he was for the war!

The Fellowship of course continued and fortunately was never disturbed in New York where its national office was located. As a member of the executive board I attended its meetings as often as possible and always found a certain healing of the spirit.

The conception of solidarity, of a new heaven and a new earth to be achieved by a band of brothers leagued against the world, is in a certain measure always found among the adherents of an unpopular cause. At the annual meeting in 1919, held at a boys school on the Hudson, it was clear from the addresses of the members and their conferences together, that the teachings of Jesus might well lead to difficult positions in regard to the industrial conflict as well as to international wars, and that the use of violence was as inadmissible in one place as in the other. One of the young clergymen there had played a leading role in the Lawrence strike, another had identified himself with a group of striking workmen in Patterson, New Jersey. No one there who had been a pacifist in war time minimized the difficulties ahead of these young men, yet they received only congratulations upon the fact that they had been able to clarify their positions and to find a clear line of action. One group was publishing a journal, another announced the opening of a new school, a third was still doing all possible to secure legal protection for men upon whom the espionage act had fallen with unusual severity.

The fourth annual meeting of the Womans Peace Party was held in Philadelphia, at the Friends Meeting House, in December 1917. Again we urged each other to promote the spirit of good will: "Let those of opposed opinions be loyal to the highest that they know, and let each understand that the other may be equally patriotic;" to work for a League of Nations and to carry on the old effort to substitute law for war.

It was interesting to observe at the Philadelphia meeting in how many ways the members of the Womans Peace Party had found "the anodyne of work" as a help to holding fast to their convictions.

The national secretary, Mrs. Mead, reported her wartime addresses in many states where, with the use of tact, she found no difficulty "even in a very super-heated atmosphere" in speaking upon "The New Preparedness," "After the War, What?" "Civic Efficiency in Wartime," and similar topics. Many others were lecturing on the food question; Miss Balch had published a book entitled "Some Approaches to the Great Settlement," but for the most part work was difficult and decreased in volume.

It was only at the very closing hour of the meeting that an agent came from the Department of Justice. The little Quaker lady who was acting as doorkeeper for the conference politely asked him to wait a few minutes, as the conference was devoting its closing minutes to silent prayer, falling into the custom of the meeting house under whose hospitable roof it was gathered. When he showed his credentials, she of course allowed him to open the door, but one look apparently satis fied him, and but for the headlines in the papers next morning we should never have known of his presence.

From the same source we learned that the agent meant to listen to my talk about "Americas Obligation and the Worlds Food Supply" in the chapel of the Friends College at Swarthmore the next day. Candor compels me to state that although he was pointed out to me I quickly forgot all about him, as I looked over the goodly group of young people, many of whom were preparing to enter the reconstruction work in France which the Friends Service Committee had inaugurated. Some of them were sent to Russia and Poland, and later on under the Hoover organization, fed the hungry in many countries of Europe. They were trying to find "the moral equivalent of war," although many of them with divided convictions and with heavy hearts.

CHAPTER VII.

PERSONAL REACTIONS DURING WAR,

After the United States had entered the war there began to appear great divergence among the many types of pacifists, from the extreme left, composed of non-resistants, through the middle-of-the-road groups, to the extreme right, who could barely be distinguished from mild militarists. There were those people, also, who although they felt keenly both the horror and the futility of war, yet hoped for certain beneficent results from the opportunities afforded by the administration of war; they were much p leased when the government took over the management of the railroads, insisting that governmental ownership had thus been pushed forward by decades; they were also sure that the War Labor Policies Board, the Coal Commission and similar war institutions would make an enormous difference in the development of the country, in short, that militarism might be used as an instrument for advanced social ends. Such justifications had their lure and one found old pacifist friends on all the war boards and even in the war department ltself. Certainly we were all eager to accept whatever progressive social changes came from the quick reorganization demanded by war, and doubtless prohibition was one of these, as the granting of woman suffrage in the majority of the belligerent nations, was another. But some of us had suspected that social advance depends as much upon the process through which it is secured as upon the result itself; if railroads are nationalized solely in order to secure rapid transit of ammunition and men to points of departure for Europe, when that governmental need no longer exists what more natural than that the railroads should no longer be managed by the government?

My temperament and habit had always kept me rather in the middle of the road; in politics as well as in social reform I had been for "the best possible." But now I was pushed far toward the left on the subject of the war and I became gradually convinced that in order to make the position of the pacifist clear it was perhaps necessary that at least a small number of us should be forced into an unequivocal position. If I sometimes regretted having gone to the Womans Congress at The Hague in 1915, or having written a book on Newer Ideals of Peace in 1911 which had made my position so conspicuously clear, certainly far oftener I was devoutly grateful that I had used such unmistakable means of expression before the time came when any spoken or written word in the interests of Peace was forbidden.

It was on my return from The Hague Congress in July, 1915, that I had my first experience of the determination on the part of the press to make pacifist activity or propaganda so absurd that it would be absolutely without influence and its authors so discredited that nothing they might say or do would be regarded as worthy of attention. I had been accustomed to newspaper men for many years and had come to regard them as a good natured fraternity, sometimes ignorant of the subject on which they asked an interview, but usually quite ready to report faithfully albeit somewhat sensationally. Hull-House had several times been the subject of sustained and inspired newspaper attacks, one, the indirect result of an exposure of the inefficient sanitary service in the Chicago Health Department had lasted for many months; I had of course known what it was to serve unpopular causes and throughout a period of campaigning for the Progressive Party I had naturally encountered the "opposition press" in various parts of the country, but this concerted and deliberate attempt at misrepresentation on the part of newspapers of all shades of opinion was quite new in my experience. After the United States entered the war, the press throughout the country systematically undertook to mis represent and malign pacifists as a recognized part of propaganda and as a patriotic duty. We came to regard this misrepresentation as part of the war technique and in fact an inevitable consequence of war itself, but we were slow in the very beginning to recognize the situation, and I found my first experience which came long before the United States entered the war rather overwhelming.

Upon our return from the Womans International Congress at The Hague in 1915, our local organization in New York City with others, notably a group of enthusiastic college men, had arranged a large public meeting in Carnegie Hall. Dr. Anna Howard Shaw presided and the United States delegates made a public report of our impressions in "war stricken Europe" and of the moral resources in the various countries we visited that might possibly be brought to bear against a continuation of the war. We had been much impressed with the fact that it was an old mans war, that the various forms of doubt and opposition to war had no method of public expression and that many of the soldiers themselves were far from enthusiastic in regard to actual fighting as a method of settling international difficulties. War was to many of them much more anachronistic than to the elderly statesmen who were primarily responsible for the soldiers presence in the trenches.

It was the latter statement which was my un doing, for in illustration of it I said that in practically every country we had visited, we had heard a certain type of young soldier say that it had been difficult for him to make the bayonet charge (enter into, actual hand to hand fighting) unless he had been stimulated; that the English soldiers had been given rum before such a charge, the Germans ether and that the French were said to use absinthe. To those who heard the address it was quite clear that it was not because the young men flinched at the risk of death but because they had to be inflamed to do the brutal work of the bayonet, such as disembowelling, and were obliged to overcome all the inhibitions of civilization.

Dr. Hamilton and I had notes for each of these statements with the dates and names of the men who had made them, and it did not occur to me that the information was new or startling. I was, however, reported to have said that no soldier could go into a bayonet charge until he was made half drunk, and this in turn was immediately commented upon, notably in a scathing letter written to the New York Times by Richard Harding Davis, as a most choice specimen of a womans sentimental nonsense. Mr. Davis himself had recently returned from Europe and at once became the defender of the heroic soldiers who were being traduced and belittled. He lent the weight of his name and his very able pen to the cause, but it really needed neither, for the misstatement was repeated, usually with scathing comment, from one end of the country to the other.

I was conscious, of course, that the story had struck athwart the popular and long-cherished conception of the nobility and heroism of the soldier as such, and it seemed to me at the time that there was no possibility of making any explanation, at least until the sensation should have somewhat subsided. I might have repeated my more sober statements with the explanation that whomsoever the pacifist held responsible for war, it was certainly not the young soldiers themselves who were, in a sense, its most touching victims, "the heroic youth of the world whom a common ideal tragically pitted against each other." Youths response to the appeal made to their self-sacrifice, to their patriotism, to their sense of duty, to their high-hearted hopes for the future, could only stir ones admiration, and we should have been dull indeed had we failed to be moved by this most moving spectacle in the world. That they had so responded to the higher appeals only confirms Ruskins statement that "we admire the soldier not because he goes forth to slay but to be slain." The fact that many of them were obliged to make a great effort to bear themselves gallantly in the final tests of "wars brutalities" had nothing whatever to do with their courage and sense of devotion. All this, of course, we had realized during our months in Europe.

After the meeting in Carnegie Hall and after an interview with President Wilson in Washington, I returned to Chicago to a public meeting arranged in the Auditorium; I was met at the train by a committee of aldermen appointed as a result of a resolution in the City Council. There was an indefinite feeling that the meeting at The Hague might turn out to be of significance, and that in such an event its chairman should have been honored by her fellow citizens. But the bayonet story had preceded me and every one was filled with great uneasiness. To be sure, a few war correspondents had come to my rescue–writing of the overpowering smell of ether preceding certain German attacks; the fact that English soldiers knew when a bayonet charge was about to be ordered because rations of rum were distributed along the trenches. Some people began to suspect that the story, exaggerated and grotesque as it had become, indicated not cowardice but merely an added sensitiveness which the modern soldier was obliged to overcome. Among the many letters on the subject which filled my mail for weeks, the bitter and abusive were from civilians or from the old men to whom war experiences had become a reminiscence, the larger number and the most understanding ones came from soldiers in active service.

Only once did I try a public explanation. After an address in Chautauqua, New York, in which I had not mentioned bayonets, I tried to remake my original statement to a young man of the associated press only to find it once more so garbled that I gave up in despair, quite unmoved by the young mans letter of apology which followed hard upon the published report of his interview.

I will confess that the mass psychology of the situation interested me even then and continued to do so until I fell ill with a serious attack of pleuro-pneumonia, which was the beginning of three years of semi-invalidism. During weeks of feverish discomfort I experienced a bald sense of social opprobrium and wide-spread misunderstanding which brought me very near to self pity, perhaps the lowest pit into which human nature can sink. Indeed the pacifist in war time, with his precious cause in the keeping of those who control the sources of publicity and consider it a patriotic duty to make all types of peace propaganda obnoxious, constantly faces two dangers. Strangely enough he finds it possible to travel from the mire of self pity straight to the barren hills of self-righteousness and to hate himself equally in both places.

From the very beginning of the great war, as the members of our group gradually became defined from the rest of the community, each one felt increasingly the sense of isolation which rapidly developed after the United States entered the war into that destroying effect of "aloneness," if I may so describe the opposite of mass conscious-ness. We never ceased to miss the unquestioning comradeship experienced by our fellow citizens during the war, nor to feel curiously outside the enchantment given to any human emotion when it is shared by millions of others. The force of the majority was so overwhelming that it seemed not only impossible to hold ones own against it, but at moments absolutely unnatural, and one secretly yearned to participate in "the folly of all mankind." Our modern democratic teaching has brought us to regard popular impulses as possessing in their general tendency a valuable capacity for evo-lutionary development. In the hours of doubt and self-distrust the question again and again arises, has the individual or a very small group, the right to stand out against millions of his fellow countrymen? Is there not a great value in mass judgment and in instinctive mass enthusiasm, and even if one were1 right a thousand times over in conviction, was he not absolutely wrong in abstaining from this communion with his fellows? The misunderstanding on the part of old friends and associates and the charge of lack of patriotism was far easier to bear than those dark periods of faint-heartedness. We gradually ceased to state our position as we became convinced that it served no practical purpose and, worse than that, often found that the immediate result was provocative.

We could not, however, lose the conviction that as all other forms of growth begin with a variation from the mass, so the moral changes in human affairs may also begin with a differing group or individual, sometimes with the one who at best is designated as a crank and a freak and in sterner moments is imprisoned as an atheist or a traitor. Just when the differing individual becomes the centro-egotist, the insane man, who must be thrown out by society for fts own protection, it is impossible to state. The pacifist was constantly brought sharply up against a genuine human trait with its biological basis, a trait founded upon the instinct to dislike, to distrust and finally to destroy the individual who differs from the mass in time of danger. Regarding this trait as the basis of self-preservation it becomes perfectly natural for the mass to call suck an individual a traitor and to insist that if he is not for the nation he is against it. To this an estimated nine million people can bear witness who have been burned as witches and heretics, not by mobs, for of the peo pie who have been "lynched" no record has been kept, but by order of ecclesiastical and civil courts.

There were moments when the pacifist yielded to the suggestion that keeping himself out of war, refusing to take part in its enthusiasms, was but pure quietism, an acute failure to adjust himself to the moral world. Certainly nothing was clearer than that the individual will was helpless and irrelevant. We were constantly told by our friends that to stand aside from the war mood of the country was to surrender all possibility of future influence, that we were committing intellectual suicide, and would never again be trusted as responsible people or judicious advisers. Who were we to differ with able statesmen, with men of sensitive conscience who also absolutely abhorred war, but were convinced that this war for the preservation of democracy would make all future wars impossible, that the priceless values of civilization which were at stake could at this moment be saved only by war? But these very dogmatic statements spurred one to alarm. Was not war in the interest of democracy for the salvation of civilization a contradiction of terms, whoever said it or however often it was repeated?

Then, too, we were always afraid of fanaticism, of preferring a consistency of theory to the conscientious recognition of the social situation, of a failure to meet life in the temper of a practical person. Every student of our time had become more or less a disciple of pragmatism and its great teachers in the United States had come out for the war and defended their positions with skill and philosophic acumen. There were moments when one longed desperately for reconciliation with ones friends and fellow citizens; in the words of Amiel, "Not to remain at variance with existence but to reach that understanding of life which enables us at least to obtain forgiveness." Solitude has always had its demons, harder to withstand than the snares of the world, and the unnatural desert into which the pacifist was summarily cast out seemed to be peopled with them. We sorely missed the contagion of mental activity, for we are all much more dependent upon our social environment and daily newspaper than perhaps any of us realize. We also doubtless encountered, although subconsciously, the temptations described by John Stuart Mill: "In respect to the persons and affairs of their own day, men insensibly adopt the modes of feeling and judgment in which they can hope for sympathy from the company they keep."

The consciousness of spiritual alienation was lost only in moments of comradeship with the like minded, which may explain the tendency of the pacifist in war time to seek his intellectual kin, his spiritual friends, wherever they might be found in his own country or abroad.

It was inevitable that in many respects the peace cause should suffer in public opinion from the efforts of groups of people who, early in the war, were convinced that the country as a whole was for peace and who tried again and again to discover a method for arousing and formulating the sentiment against war. I was ill and out of Chicago when the Peoples Council held a national convention there, which was protected by the city police but threatened with dispersion by the state troops, who, however, arrived from the capital several hours after the meeting had adjourned. The incident was most sensational and no one was more surprised than many of the members of the Peoples Council who thus early in the war had supposed that they were conducting a perfectly legitimate convention. The incident gave tremendous "copy" in a city needing rationalizing rather than sensationalizing at that moment. There is no doubt that the shock and terror of the "anarchist riots" occurring in Chicago years ago have left their traces upon the nervous system of the city somewhat as a nervous shock experienced in youth will long afterwards determine the action of a mature man under widely different circumstances.

On the whole, the New York groups were much more active and throughout the war were allowed much more freedom both of assembly and press, although later a severe reaction followed expressed through the Lusk Committee and other agencies. Certainly neither city approximated the freedom of London and nothing surprised me more in 1915 and again in 1919 than the freedom of speech permitted there.

We also read with a curious eagerness the steadily increasing number of books published from time to time during the war, which brought a renewal of ones faith or at least a touch of comfort. These books broke through that twisting and suppressing of awkward truths, which was encouraged and at times even ordered by the censorship. Such manipulation of news and motives was doubtless necessary in the interest of war propaganda if the people were to be kept in a fighting mood. Perhaps the most vivid books came from France, early from Romain Holland, later from Barbusse, although it was interesting to see how many people took the latters burning indictment of war merely as a further incitement against the enemy. On the scientific side were the frequent writings of David Starr Jordan and the remarkable book of Nicolai on "The Biology of War." The latter enabled one, at least in ones own mind, to refute the pseudo-scientific statement that war was valuable in securing the survival of the fittest. Nicolai insisted that primitive man must necessarily have been a peaceful and social animal and that he developed his intelligence through the use of the tool, not through the use of the weapon; it was the primeval community which made the evolution of man possible, and cooperation among men is older and more primitive than mass combat which is an outgrowth of the much later property instinct. No other species save ants, who also possess property, fights in masses against other masses of its own kind. War is in fact not a natural process and not a struggle for existence in the evolutionary sense. He illustrated the evolutionary survival of the fittest by two tigers inhabiting the same jungle or feeding ground, the one who has the greater skill and strength as a hunter survives and the other starves, but the strong one does not go out to kill the weak one, as the war propagandist implied; or by two varieties of mice living in the same field or barn; in the biological struggle, the variety which grows a thicker coat survives the winter while the other variety freezes to extinction, but if one variety of mice should go forth to kill the other, it would be absolutely abnormal and quite outside the evolutionary survival which is based on the adjustment of the organism to its environment. George Nas-myths book on Darwinism and the Social Order was another clear statement of the mental confusion responsible for the insistence that even a biological progress is secured through war. Mr. Brailsford wrote constantly on the economic results of the war and we got much comfort from John Hobsons "Toward International Government," which gave an authoritative account of the enormous amount of human activity actually carried on through international organizations of all sorts, many of them under governmental control. Lowes Dickensons books, especially the spirited challenge in "The Choice Before Us," left his readers with the distinct impression that "war is not inevitable but proceeds from definite and removable causes." From every such book the pacifist was forced to the conclusion that none save those interested in the realization of an idea are in a position to bring it about and that if one found himself the unhappy possessor of an unpopular conviction, there was nothing for it but to think as clearly as he was able and be in a position to serve his country as soon as it was possible for him to do so.

But with or without the help of good books a hideous sensitiveness remained, for the pacifist, like the rest of the world, has developed a high degree of suggestibility, sharing that consciousness of the feelings, the opinions and the customs of his own social group which is said to be an inheri tance from an almost pre-human past. An instinct which once enabled the man-pack to survive when it was a question of keeping together or of perishing off the face of the earth, is perhaps not underdeveloped in any of us. There is a distinct physical as well as moral strain when this instinct is steadily suppressed or at least ignored.

The large number of deaths among the older pacifists in all the warring nations can probably be traced in some measure to the peculiar strain which such maladjust-ment implies. More than the normal amount of nervous energy must be consumed in holding ones own in a hostile world. These older men, Kier Hardie and Lord Courtney in England, Jenkin Lloyd Jones, Rauchen-busch, Washington Gladden in the United States, Lammasch and Fried in Austria, had been honored by their fellow citizens because of marked ability to interpret and understand them. Suddenly to find every public utterance wilfully misconstrued, every attempt at normal relationship repudiated, must react in a baffled suppression which is health-destroying even if we do not accept the mechanistic explanation of the human system. Certainly by the end of the war we were able to understand, although our group certainly did not endorse the statement of Cobden, one of the most convinced of all internationalists: "I made up my mind during the Crimean War that if ever I lived in the time of another great war of a similar kind between England and another power, I would not as a public man open my mouth on the subject, so convinced am I that appeals to reason, conscience or interest have no force whatever on parties engaged in war, and that exhaustion on one or both sides can alone bring a contest of physical force to an end."

On the other hand there were many times when we stubbornly asked ourselves, what after all, has maintained the human race on this old globe despite all the calamities of nature and all the tragic failings of mankind, if not faith in new possibilities, and courage to advocate them. Doubtless many times these new possibilities were declared by a man who, quite unconscious of courage, bore the "sense of being an exile, a condemned criminal, a fugitive from mankind." Did every one so feel who, in order to travel on his own proper path had been obliged to leave the traditional highway? The pacifist, during the period of the war could answer none of these questions but he was sick at heart from causes which to him were hidden and impossible to analyze. He was at times devoured by a veritable dissatisfaction with life. Was he thus bearing his share of blood-guiltiness, the morbid sense of contradiction and inexplicable suicide which modern war implies? We certainly had none of the internal contentment of the doctrinnaire, the ineffable solace of the self-righteous which was imputed to us. No one knew better than we how feeble and futile we were against the impregnable weight of public opinion, the appalling imperviousness, the coagulation of motives, the universal confusion of a world at war. There was scant solace to be found in this type of statement: "The worth of every conviction consists precisely in the steadfastness with which it is held," perhaps because we suffered from the fact that we were no longer living in a period of dogma and were therefore in no position to announce our sense of security I We were well aware that the modern liberal having come to conceive truth of a kind which must vindicate itself in practice, finds it hard to hold even a sincere and mature opinion which from the very nature of things can have no justification in works. The pacifist in war time is literally starved of any gratification of that natural desire to have his own decisions justified by his fellows.

That, perhaps, was the crux of the situation. We slowly became aware that our affirmation was regarded as pure dogma. We were thrust into the position of the doctrinnaire, and although, had we been permitted, we might have cited both historic and scientific tests of our so-called doctrine of Peace, for the moment any sanction even by way of illustration was impossible.

It therefore came about that ability to hold out against mass suggestion, to honestly differ from the convictions and enthusiasms of ones best friends did in moments of crisis come to depend upon the categorical belief that a mans primary allegiance is to his vision of the truth and that he is under obligation to affirm it.

CHAPTER VIII IN EUROPE DURING THE ARMISTICE In line with a resolution passed at our Hague Congress in 1915, "that our next Congress should be held at the time and place of the official Peace Conference," each of the national sections had appointed a committee of five, who were to start for the place of the Peace Conference as soon as the arrangements were announced. They were then to cable back to the selected twenty delegates and ten alternates in each country, who were to follow as quickly as preparations could be made. It was assumed in 1915, not only by ourselves, but largely by the rest of the world, that the Peace Conference would be held in a neutral country, probably at The Hague, and that both sides would be represented there.

In planning a congress of women it was borne in mind that the official Conference at the end of the war determining the terms of peace would be largely composed of diplomats who are necessarily bound by the traditional conventions which have so long dominated all intercourse between nations. Because in every country such men are 152 seldom representative of modern social thought and the least responsive to changing ideas, it was considered supremely important that when the conference of diplomats should come together, other groups should convene in order to urge the importance of certain interests which have hitherto been inarticulate in international affairs. This need had been recognized not only by the women but by international organizations of labor, by the Zionists and similar groups, who were also planning to hold Congresses at the same time and in the same place as the official Peace Conference After the War.

The tremendous movement for a League of Nations, the gathering together of experts and scholars as aids to the official Peace Commissioners had of course all developed after our Congress at The Hague in 1915, but all the more did we hope for a great spiritual awakening in international affairs. We recalled that it was at the Congress of Vienna in 1815 after the Napoleonic wars that the nations represented there, as part of their overwhelming demand for a more highly moralized future, insisted that the diplomats should make international provision for abolishing the slave trade.

When it was announced that the Peace Confer-, ence would assemble in Paris all the plans for our Womans Congress fell through. It was neces sary, of course, for us to meet in a neutral country as naturally the women from the Central Powers could not go to France. This inevitable change of place involved much cabling and delay, and there were also some difficulties in regard to passports even for neutral Switzerland.

The group of American delegates arriving in Paris at Easter, 1919 found that the English passports had been delayed and that the brilliant president of our French Section and her fellow officers had been refused theirs. After various meetings in Paris, at which the French, English and American sections were well represented, the Congress was finally arranged for May 12, at Zurich. Curiously enough, after our many delays, we at last met in the very week when the Peace Conference in Paris had become enlarged beyond the membership of the Allied and neutral nations by receiving the delegates from the Central Powers, and when in a sense the official Peace Conference as such had formally begun. Our fortnight of delay in Paris was spent in conference with our French colleagues, in interviews with various persons connected both with the Peace Conference and the Food Administration, and by some of us in a five-days visit to the devastated regions, which was made by automobile, kindly arranged for us by the American Red Cross.

Day after day as rain, snow and sleet fell steadily from a leaden sky, we drove through lands laid waste and still encumbered by mounds of munitions, exploded shells, broken down tanks and incredibly huge tangles of rusty barbed wire. The ground was furrowed in all directions by trenches and shell holes, we passed through ruined towns and villages in which no house had been left standing, although at times a grey head would emerge from a cellar which had been rudely roofed with bits of corrugated iron. It was always the old people who had come back first, for they least of all could brook the life of refugees. There had not yet been time to gather the dead into cemeteries, but at Vimy Ridge colored troops from the United States were digging rows of graves for the bodies being drawn toward them in huge trucks. In the Argonne we still saw clusters of wooden crosses surmounting the heaps of clay, each cross with its metal tag for inscription.

I had a personal interest in these graves for my oldest nephew had fallen in the Argonne. We searched for his grave through one long afternoon but, owing to the incompleteness of our map and the fact that there was no living soul to consult in the village nearest the farm on which the battle had been fought, we failed to find it. We met other people on the same errand, one a French Cure who knew the ground with a sad intimacy.

We spent the following night at the headquarters of the reconstruction work of the Friends Service Committee in devastated France, where the work of both the English and American units was being supervised by Edward Harvey, who had been Canon Barnetts successor as Warden, of Toynbee Hall. After an evening of talk to which the young men had come in from all the outlying villages where they were constructing temporary houses for the refugees who had returned, or plowing the fields for those who had not yet arrived, or supplying necessities to those who had come back too ill to begin their regular course of living, four of us who had long been identified with settlements sat by a small open fire and tried to disentangle the moral situation into which the war had thrown those who could not consider it-legitimate, yet felt acutely the call to service on behalf of its victims and the full measure of pity for the colossal devastation and helpless misery. In the morning one of the Friends went with us to the region we had searched the day before, and although we early abandoned the motor in the shell wrecked road, he finally found the farm and grave we sought, the third in one of three long rows.

On May 6, 1915, the Executive Committee of the Womans International Committee for Permanent Peace met in Zurich to prepare the agenda of the Congress. The members represented groups of women who, living in fourteen different nations of the neutral, the Entente and the Central Powers, had found themselves opposed to the full tide of public opinion throughout the war. That a curious fellowship had developed between these widely scattered groups was revealed from time to time when committee members recounted, merely by way of explanation in regard to incomplete records or absent delegates, such similar experiences with governmental espionage as to demonstrate without doubt that war methods are identical in all nations. Without explanation or asseveration we also discovered how like-minded we were when resolutions on the same subject, coming in from one country after another, were so similar in intent that the five sub-committees who sorted and combined and translated the material were often perplexed to decide which resolution most clearly expressed that which was common to them all, which one best reflected something of what we had learned and hoped through the poignant suffering of the past five years. In one sense these resolutions gave a cross-cut section,–although in a business-like form, as it were–of the hopes maturing in many countries, including those so lately at war, for "permanent arrangements that justice shall be rendered and peace maintained." We knew that there would be diffi culties in holding an international Congress so soon after the war, but in all humility of spirit we claimed that we essayed the task free from any rancorous memories, from wilful misunderstanding or distrust of so-called enemies.

Therefore in reply to the often repeated prediction that the Congress was premature and that the attempt would end in disaster, which was made not only in the United States but still oftener by American women in Paris who were sensitive to the hostility still prevailing during the peace negotiations, we could only state our conviction that the women eligible to membership in the Congress had suffered too much during the war, had been too close to the clarifying spirit of reality to indulge in any sentimental or unconsidered statements.

Yet inevitably we felt a certain restraint–self-consciousness would perhaps be a better word–when we considered seeing the "alien enemy" face to face. I imagine many of the experiences were similar to my own when walking the streets of Zurich the day we arrived I turned a corner and suddenly met one of the Austrian women who had been a delegate to The Hague Congress and had afterwards shown us every courtesy in Vienna when we presented our Neutral Conference plan. She was so shrunken and changed that I had much difficulty in identifying her with the beautiful woman I had seen three years before. She was not only emaciated as by a wasting illness, looking as if she needed immediate hospital care–she did in fact die three months after her return to Vienna–but her face and artists hands were covered with rough red blotches due to the long use of soap substitutes, giving her a cruelly scalded appearance. My first reaction was one of overwhelming pity and alarm as I suddenly discovered my friend standing at the very gate of death. This was quickly followed by the same sort of indignation I had first felt in the presence of the starving children at Lille. What were we all about that such things were allowed to happen in a so-called civilized world? Certainly all extraneous differences fell from us as we stood together in the spring sunshine and spoke of the coming Congress which, feeble as it was, yet gave a demonstration that a few women were to be found in each country who could not brook that such a state of affairs should go unchallenged. At the evening meeting preceding the opening of the Congress this dying woman told us that many Austrian women had resented not so much the starvation itself as the fact that day after day they had been obliged to keep their minds steadily on the subject of procuring food until all other objects for living were absolutely excluded. To the horror and anxieties of war had been added the sordid- ness of sheer animal hunger with its inhibitions. She spoke in the white marble hall of the University of Zurich. The same meeting was addressed by a German delegate and by an American who had both come back to the University which had given them doctors degrees. What a welcome they received from the Swiss people! We had almost forgotten what it was like to be in a neutral country where it entailed no odium to be a pacifist.

After the formal opening of the Congress had been disposed of, the first resolution proposed was on the famine and blockade. It was most eloquently presented by Mrs. Pethwick Lawrence of England and went through without a dissenting vote:

"This International Congress of Women regards the famine, pestilence and unemployment extending throughout the great tracts of Central and Eastern Europe and into Asia as a disgrace to civilization.

"It therefore urges the Governments of all the Powers assembled at the Peace Conference immediately to develop the interallied organizations formed for purposes of war into an international organization for purposes of peace, so that the resources of the world–food, raw materials, finance, transport–shall be made available for the relief of the peoples of all countries from famine and pestilence.

"To this end it urges that immediate action be taken:

"1. To raise the blockade; and

"2. If there is insufficiency of food or transport;

"a. To prohibit the use of transport from one country to another for the conveyance of luxuries until the necessaries of life are supplied to all peoples;

"b. To ration the people of every country so that the starving may be fed.

"The Congress believes that only immediate international action on these lines can save humanity and bring about the permanent reconciliation and union of the peoples."

The resolution in full was telegraphed to Paris and we received a prompt reply from President Wilson. The public reception of this telegram was one of the most striking moments of the Congress and revealed once more the reverence with which all Europe regarded the President of the United States. As the university hall was too small for the increasing attendance, we held our last evening meetings in the largest church in the city. As I stood in the old-fashioned high pulpit to announce the fact that a telegram had been received from President Wilson, there fell a hush, a sense of tension on the great audience that is difficult to describe. It was as if out of the con fusion and misery of Europe one authoritative voice was about to be heard. Although the telegram itself but expressed sympathy with our famine resolution, and regret that the Paris Conference could not act upon its suggestions, there arose from the audience a sigh of religious resignation, as if a good man were doing his best and in the end must succeed.

As the Congress had received through our press correspondent an advance copy of the treaty and was in actual session the very day the treaty was made public, we were naturally in a position to be the very first public body to discuss its terms. We certainly spoke out unequivocally in a series of resolutions, beginning as follows:

"This International Congress of Women expresses its deep regret that the Terms of Peace proposed at Versailles should so seriously violate the principles upon which alone a just and lasting peace can be secured, and which the democracies of the world had come to accept."

"By guaranteeing the fruits of the secret treaties to the conquerors, the Terms of Peace tacitly sanction secret diplomacy, deny the principles of self-determination, recognize the right of the victors to the spoils of war, and create all over Europe discords and animosities, which can only lead to future wars.

"By the demand for the disarmament of one set of belligerents only, the principle of justice is violated and the rule of force continued.

"By the financial and economic proposals a hundred million people of this genera-tion in the heart of Europe are condemned to poverty, disease and despair which must result in the spread of hatred and anarchy within each nation.

"With a deep sense of responsibility this Congress strongly urges the Allied and Associated Governments to accept such amendments of the Terms, as shall bring the peace into harmony with those principles first enumerated by President Wilson upon the faithful carrying out of which the honor of the Allied peoples depends."

It was creditable to the patience of the peace makers in Paris that they later received our delegation and allowed us to place the various resolutions in their hands, but we inevitably encountered much bitter criticism from the Allied press. Only slowly did public opinion reach a point of view similar to ours: Keynes epoch-making book was not published until a year later, but so widely was his position ratified that on the second celebration of Armistice day in Kingsbury House in London at a meeting of ex-soldiers and sailors, one of the latter who had been sorely wounded, spoke as follows: "For every man who a year ago knew and said that the Peace Treaty was immoral in con ception and would be disastrous, there are thousands who say it now."

There was much discussion at the Zurich Congress on the League of Nations; the first committee made a majority and minority report, another committee reconciled them and resolutions were finally passed but the Zurich Congress took no definite position for or against the League of Nations. As the formal organization of the League was open to change by the Peace Conference still sitting, a number of careful suggestions were formulated and sent to Paris by a special committee from the Congress. Two of the English members discussed them with Lord Robert Cecil, I saw Colonel House several times, our committee through the efforts of an Italian member was received by Signor Orlando and we also had a hearing at the Quai dorsay with the French minister of foreign affairs, and with the delegates from other countries. In Paris at that time the representatives of the smaller nations were already expressing their disappointment in the League but its proponents were elated over its adoption and hopeful for the future. They all received our resolutions politely and sometimes discussed them at length, but only a few of the journalists and "experts" were enthusiastic about them.

Throughout the meetings of the Zurich Congress the delegates, secure in their sense of good will and mutual understanding, spoke freely not only of their experiences during the trial of war, but also of the methods which they were advocating for the difficult period of social and industrial re-adjustment following the war. Some of our delegates represented nations in which revolutions with and without bloodshed had already taken place. The members of our organization had stood against the use of armed force in such domestic crises as definitely as they had protested against its use in international affairs. The pacifists had already played this role in the revolutions in Bavaria, in Austria, in Hungary. Having so soon come together under the shadow of the great war itself, we had an opportunity to hear early of the courageous and intelligent action taken by our own groups in the widespread war after the war.

The Congress ending with a banquet given by the town officials, was attended by delegates from fifteen different countries, many of whom had come under great difficulties. Despite sharp differences as to terms in the Treaty, the meetings were absolutely harmonious and many delegates confessed to each other that they felt as if they were passing through a rare spiritual experience. In addition to a long list of resolutions on international affairs, a womans charter and an education program were drawn up. The name of the or ganization was changed to "Womans International League for Peace and Freedom" and Geneva, as the seat of the League of Nations, was made the headquarters. Emily Balch, from the United States, a professor of economics in Welles-ley College became secretary, agreeing to remain in Europe for the following two years.

On our return to Paris there were many symptoms of the malaise and confusion for which the peace terms were held responsible although it would be difficult to say how much of it was the inevitable aftermath of war. In the midst of it all only the feeding of the hungry seemed to offer the tonic of beneficent activity. During our stop at Paris in May we had talked with Dr. Nansen, who was keen on the prospect of entering Russia for the sake of feeding the women and children, but upon our return we found that the Nansen plan had been indefinitely postponed in spite of the popular reports that thousands of people in the aftermath of war were starving in the industrial centers of Russia. Mr. Hoovers office seemed to be the one reasonable spot in the midst of the widespread confusion; the great maps upon the wall recorded the available food resources and indicated fleets of ships carrying wheait from Australia to Finland or corn from the port of New York to Fiume. And yet even at that moment the food blockade, hitherto regarded as a war meas ure, was being applied both to Hungary and Russia as pressure against their political arrangements, foreboding sinister possibilities. The Zurich Congress had made a first protest against this unfair use of the newly formulated knowledge of the worlds food supply and of a centralized method for its distribution. There was a soviet regime in Hungary during our meeting in Zurich. Of our two delegates from Hungary, one was in sympathy with it and one was not, but they both felt hotly against the blockade which had been instituted against Hungary as an attempt to settle the question of the form of government through the starvation of the people.

On our return to Paris after the Zurich Congress, Dr. Hamilton and I accepted an invitation from the American Friends Service Committee to go into Germany. In explanation of our journey it may be well to quote from a "minute" passed at a meeting held in Devonshire House, London, the central office of the Society of Friends, July 4th, 1919: "We are thankful to learn that certain members of the Religious Society of Friends are now proceeding to Germany under a deep sense of the need which exists for mutual friendly intercourse and fellowship between those who all belong to the same great human family and who have been separated during these sad years of war.

"Our friends are traveling on behalf of the Committee which has under its care the arrangements for sending Gifts of Love to Germany, in the form of food, clothes and other necessaries,—a work that is shared in by many other persons not associated with Friends in membership."

The four English members of the Committee traveled through the occupied region, entered Germany via Cologne, and reached Berlin July 6th; the three American members who traveled through Holland and crossed the border on the first civilian passports issued there since the signing of peace, arrived in Berlin July 7th. Dr. Aletta Jacobs, who had been asked as a neutral to make observations on health conditions in Germany, was the fourth member of the second party. Dr. Elizabeth Rotten, of Berlin, who had been acting as the representative in Germany of the work of the English Friends and was also head of the Educational Committee of the Germany Association for the Promotion of the League of Nations, was naturally our guide and advisor.

We were received everywhere in a fine spirit of courtesy. Doctors, nurses and city officials, who were working against tuberculosis, to keep children healthy, to prevent youthful crime and foster education, had long passed the mood of bitterness. What they were facing was the shipwreck of a nation and they had no time for resent ments. They realized that if help did not come quickly and abundantly, the coming generation in Germany was largely doomed to early death or, at best, to a handicapped life.

We had, of course, seen something of the widespread European starvation before we went into Germany; our first view in Europe of starved children was in the city of Lille in Northern France, where the school children were being examined for tuberculosis. We had already been told that forty per cent of the children of school age in Lille had open tuberculosis and that the remaining sixty per cent were practically all suspects. As we entered the door of a large school room, we saw at the other end of the room a row of little boys, from six to ten years of age, passing slowly in front of the examining physician. The children were stripped to the waist and our first impression was of a line of moving skeletons; their little shoulder blades stuck straight out, the vertebrae were all perfectly distinct as were their ribs, and their bony arms hung limply at their sides. To add to the gruesome effect not a sound was to be heard, for the French physician had lost his voice as a result of shell shock during the first bombardment of Lille. He therefore whispered his instructions to the children as he applied his stethoscope and the children, thinking it was some sort of game, all whispered back to him. It was in credibly pathetic and unreal and we could but accept the doctors grave statement that only by a system of careful superfeeding, could any of these boys grow into normal men. We had also seen starved children in Switzerland: six hundred Viennese children arriving in Zurich to be guests in private households. As they stood upon the station platforms without any of the bustle and chatter naturally associated with a large number of children, we had again that painful impression of listlessness as of a mortal illness; we saw the winged shoulder blades standing out through their meagre clothing, the little thin legs which scarcely supported the emaciated bodies. The committee of Swiss women was offering them cakes and chocolates, telling them of the children at home who were waiting for them, but there was little response because there was no vitality with which to make it.

We were reminded of these children week after week as we visited Berlin, or Frankfort am Main, or the cities of Saxony and the villages throughout the Erzgebirge in which the children had been starved throughout the long period of the war and of the armistice. Perhaps an experience in Leipzig was typical when we visited a public playground in which several hundred children were having a noonday meal consisting for each of a pint of "war soup," composed of war meal stirred into a pint of hot water. The war meal was, as always, made with a foundation of rye or wheat flour to which had been added ground vegetables or sawdust in order to increase its bulk. The children would have nothing more to eat until supper, for which many of the mothers had saved the entire daily ration of bread because, as they sometimes told us, they hoped thus to avert the hardest thing they had to bear; hearing the children whimper and moan for hours after they were put to bed because they were too hungry to go to sleep.

These Leipzig children were quite as listless as all the others we had seen; when the playground director announced prizes for the best gardens, they were utterly indifferent; only when he said he hoped by day after tomorrow to give them milk in their soup did they break out into the most ridiculous, feeble little cheer ever heard. The city physician, who was with us, challenged the playground director as to his ability to obtain the milk, to which the director replied that he was not sure that he could, but that there was a prospect for it, and that the children must have something to hope for, that that was the prerogative of the young. With this uncertain hope we left them to visit day nurseries, child welfare stations, schools and orphanages where the midday meal was practically the same war soup. We were told by probation officers and charity workers of starved children who stole the family furniture and clothing, books and kitchen utensils in order to sell them for food, who pulled unripe potatoes and turnips from the fields for miles surrounding the cities, to keep themselves alive.

Our experiences in the midst of widespread misery, did not differ from those of thousands of other Americans who were bent upon succor and relief and our vivid and compelling impressions of widespread starvation were confirmed by the highest authorities. Mr. Hoover had recently declared that, owing to diminished food production in Europe, approximately 100,000,000 Europeans were then dependent upon imported food. Sir George Paish, the British economist, repeated the statement when he said that 100,000,000 persons in Europe were facing starvation. All this was made much worse by the rapid decline in the value of European money in the markets of the world.

One turned instinctively to the newly created League of Nations. Could it have considered this multitude of starving children as its concrete problem, feeding them might have been the quickest way to restore the divided European nations to human and kindly relationship. Was all this devastation the result of hypernationalism and might not the very recognition of a human obligation irrespective of national boundaries form the natural beginning of better international relationships?

My entire experience in Europe in 1915 was in marked contrast to my impressions received thirty-four years earlier, in 1885. Nationalism was also the great word then, but with quite another content. At that moment in all political matters the great popular word had been Unity; a coming together into new national systems of little states which had long been separated. The words of Mazzini, who had died scarcely a decade before, were constantly on the lips of ardent young orators, the desire to unite, to overcome differences, to accentuate likenesses, was everywhere a ruling influence in political affairs. Italy had become united under Victor Emanuel; the first Kaiser and Bismarck ruled over a German Empire made of many minor states. It rather smacked of learning, in those days, to use the words Slavophile and Panslavic, but we knew that the movement stood for unity in the remoter parts of Europe where Bohemia was the most vocal, although she talked less of a republic of her own than of her desire to unite with her fellow Slavs. The most striking characteristic of all these nationalistic movements had been their burning humanitarianism, a sense that the new groupings were but a preparation for a wider synthesis, that a federation of at least the European states was a possibility in the near future.

In 1885 I had seen nationalistic fervor pulling scattered people together, but in 1919 it seemed equally effective in pushing those apart who had once been combined—a whole ring of states was pulling out of Mother Russia, Bavaria was threatening to leave Germany, and Italy, in the name of nationalism was separating a line of coast with its hinterland of Slavs, from their newly found brethren. Whereas nationalism thirty years earlier had seemed generous and inclusive, stressing likenesses, it now appeared dogmatic and ruthless, insisting upon historic prerogatives quite independent of the popular will. Had the nationalistic fervor become overgrown and over-reached itself, or was it merely for the moment so self-assertive that the creative impulse was submerged into the possessive instinct? Had nationalism become dogmatic and hardened in thirty-five years? It was as if I had left a group of early Christians and come back into a flourishing mediasval church holding great possessions and equipped with well tried methods of propaganda. The early spontaneity had changed into an authoritative imposition of power. One received the impression everywhere in that moment when nationalism was so tremendously stressed, that the nation was demanding worship and devotion for its own sake similar to that of the mediaeval church, as if it existed for its own ends of growth and power irrespective of the tests of reality. It demanded unqualified obedience, denounced as heretics all who differed, insisted that it alone had the truth, and exhibited all the well known signs of dogmatism, including a habit of considering ordinary standards inapplicable to a certain line of conduct if it were inspired by motives beyond reproach.

We saw arriving in Rotterdam, from the German colonies in Africa and the Pacific, hundreds of German families who had been driven from their pioneer homes and their colonial business undertakings, primarily because they belonged to the outlaw nation; in many of the railroad stations in Germany there were posted directions for the fugitives coming from Posen, from Alsace, from the new Czecho-Slovakia and from the Danzig corridor. As we had opportunity to learn of their experiences, they told of prohibition of language, of the forced sale of real estate, of the confiscation of business, of the expulsion from university faculties and the alienation of old friends. There was something about it all that was curiously anachronistic like the expulsion of the Jews from Spain, or Cromwells drive through Ireland when the Catholics took refuge in the barren west country, or of the action by which France had made herself poorer for generations when she banished her Huguenots. It is as if nationalism, through the terms of the Peace Conference itself, had fallen back into an earlier psychology, exhibiting a blind intolerance which does not properly belong to these later centuries.

After all, the new Nationalism–even counting its rise as beginning three hundred years ago–is still in its early history. It might be possible for its representatives to meet in frank and fearless discussion of its creeds as the early church in its first centuries called its Ecumenical Councils.

These creeds would easily divide into types: the hypernationalism, if one may call it such, of the suppressed nations, as Ireland, Poland or Bohemia; the imperialistic nationalism of empires like Great Britain in which colonial expansion had become the normal expression and is no longer challenged as a policy; the revolutionary type, such as Russia attempting an economic state. Every nation would show traces of all types of nationalism, and it would be found that all types have displayed the highest devotion to their ideals.

It is possible that such a hypothetical Council would discover that as the greatest religious war came at the very moment when men were deciding that they no longer cared intensely for the theological creeds for which they had long been fighting, so this devastating war may have come at a similar moment in regard to national dogmas. The world, at the very verge of the creation of the League of Nations may be entering an era when the differing types will no longer suppress each other but live together in a fuller and richer comity than has ever before been possible. But the League of Nations must find a universal motive which shall master the overstimulated nationalism so characteristic of Europe after the war.

We came home late in August, inevitably disappointed in the newly formed League, but eager to see what would happen when "the United States came in!"

CHAPTER IX

THE AFTERMATH OF WAR

A Few months after our return from Europe the annual meeting of the Womans Peace Party was held in Philadelphia, again at the Friends Meeting House. The reports showed that during the war the state branches had modified their activities in various ways. The Massachusetts branch had carried on war relief of many kinds, such as the operation of a plant for desiccating vegetables. The New York Branch on the other hand, had become more radical and in defense of its position published a monthly Journal entitled The Four Winds, which was constantly challenged by the Federal authorities. The annual meeting adopted the somewhat formidable name of Womans International League for Peace and Freedom, Section for the United States, the Zurich resolutions were accepted for substance of doctrine and recommended for study.

We made a careful restatement of our policies, but the bald outline gave no more than a hint of the indomitable faith of the women gathered there who, after nearly five years of anxiety and 178 of hope deferred, still solemnly agreed to renew the struggle against the war system and to work for a wider comity of nations.

Two of the new officers, Mrs. Lucy Biddle Lewis and Mrs. Wm. I. Hull, belonged to the Society of Friends, without whose help it would have been hard to survive. It is difficult for me adequately to express my admiration for Mrs. Anna Garlin Spencer who was president of the National League during the most difficult period of its existence. With the help of two able executive secretaries, she deliberately revived an organization devoted to the discredited cause of Peace at a moment when the established peace societies with which she had been long connected had carefully stripped themselves of all activity.

In some respects it was more difficult at that time to be known as a pacifist than it had been during the war, and if any of us had ever imagined that our troubles would be over when the war ended, we were doomed to disappointment. There were many illustrations of our continued unpopularity. In the early days of the armistice, for instance, a group of German women, distressed over such terms as the demand for the immediate restoration of 3000 milch cows to Belgium, cabled to Mrs. Wilson at the White House and also to me. My cable was never delivered and I knew nothing but what the newspapers reported con cerning it, although the incident started an interminable chain of comment and speculation as to why I should have been selected, none of which stumbled upon the simple truth that I had presided over a Congress at The Hague attended by two of the signatories of the cable.

The incident, however, was but a foretaste of the suspicions and misinterpretations resulting from the efforts of Miss Hamilton and myself to report conditions in Germany and so far as possible to secure contributions to the fund the Friends Service Committee in Philadelphia was collecting for German and Austrian children. There was no special odium attached to the final report which we made to the Friends upon our return nor upon its wide distribution in printed form; it was also comparatively easy to speak to the International Committee for the Promotion of Friendship between the Churches and to similar bodies, but when it came to addressing audiences of German descent, so-called "German-Americans," the trouble began. The first Chicago meeting of this kind was carefully arranged, "opened with prayer" by a popular clergyman and closed by a Catholic priest, and it went through without difficulty although, of course, no word of it appeared in any Chicago newspaper printed in English. Milwaukee, St. Louis and Cleveland, however, were more difficult, although my theme was purely humanitarian with no word of politics. I told no audience that our passports had been viseed in Frankfort in the city hall flying a red flag, that housing space was carefully proportioned with reference to the need of the inhabitants and other such matters, which would have shocked the audience of prosperous German-Americans quite as much as any one else. We always told these audiences as we told many others who invited us, about the work of the Friends Service Committee in Northern France and over widespread portions of Central and Eastern Europe irrespective of national boundaries. Some money was always sent to Philadelphia for Germany but quite often it was carefully marked for one of the Allied countries in which the Friends Service Committee was also at work. I was equally grateful for those contributions but I often longed to hear some one suggest that "to feed thine enemy if he hunger" might lead us back to normal relations with him, or to hear one of the many clergymen pray that we might forgive our enemies. No such sentiment was uttered in my hearing during that winter, although in the early Spring I was much cheered at a meeting in Denver when a club woman quoted apropos of feeding German children, from Bojers "The Great Hunger": "I sow corn in the field of mine enemy in order to prove the existence of God."

It was a period or pronounced reaction, characterized by all sorts of espionage, of wholesale raids, arrests and deportations. Liberals everywhere soon realized that a contest was on all over the world for the preservation of that hard won liberty which since the days of Edmund Burke had come to mean to the civilized world not only security in life and property but in opinion as well. Many people had long supposed liberalism to be freedom to know and to sayv not what was popular or convenient or even what was patriotic, but what they held to be true. But those very liberals came to realize that a distinct aftermath of the war was the dominance of the mass over the individual to such an extent that it constituted a veritable revolution in our social relationships. Every part of the country had its own manifestations of suspicion and distrust which to a surprising degree fastened upon the immigrants. These felt, some of them with good reason, that they were being looked upon with suspicion and regarded as different from the rest of the world; that whatever happened in this country that was hard to understand was put off upon them, as if they alone were responsible. In such a situation they naturally became puzzled and irritated. With all the rest of the world America fell back 1nto the old habit of judging men, not by their individual merits or capacities, but by the categories of race and religion, thrusting them back into the part of the world in which they had been born. Many of the immigrants, Poles, Bohemians and Croatians, were eager to be called by their new names. They were keenly alive to the fresh start made in Poland, in Czecho-Slovakia, in Jugo-Slavia and in other parts of Eastern and Southern Europe. They knew, of course, of the redistributions in land, of the recognition of peasant proprietorship occurring not only in the various countries in which actual revolutions had taken place as in Hungary and Russia, but in other countries such as Roumania, where there had been no violent revolution. These immigrants were very eager to know what share they themselves might have in these great happenings if they returned. They longed to participate in the founding of a new state which might guarantee the liberties in search of which they themselves had come to America. They were also anxious about untoward experiences which might have befallen their kinsfolk in those remote countries. For five years many of them had heard nothing directly from their families and their hearts were wrung over the possible starvation of their parents and sometimes of their wives and children.

Had we as citizens of the United States made a widespread and generous response to this overwhelming anxiety, much needed results might have accrued to ourselves; our sympathy and aid given to their kinsmen in the old world might have served to strengthen the bonds between us and the foreigners living within our borders. There was a chance to restore the word alien to a righteous use and to end its service as a term of reproach. To ignore the natural anxiety of the Russians and to fail to understand their inevitable resentment against an unauthorized blockade, to account for their "restlessness" by all sorts of fantastic explanations was to ignore a human situation which was full of possibilities for a fuller fellowship and understanding.

It was stated in the Senate that one and a half million European immigrants had applied in the winter of 19 and 20 for return passports. In one small Western city in which 800 Russians were living, 275 went to the Western Coast hoping for an opportunity to embark for Siberia and thus to reach Russia. Most of them were denied passports and the enforced retention of so many people constantly made for what came to be called social unrest. We would sometimes hear a Russian say, "When I was in the old country I used to dream constantly of America, and of the time I might come here, but now I go about with the same longing in my heart for Russia, and am. homesick to go back to her." In Chicago many of those who tried in vain to return, began to prepare themselves in all sorts of ways for usefulness in the new Russian state. Because Russia needed skilled mechanics they themselves founded schools in applied mathematics, in mechanical drawing, in pattern work, in automobiling.

It was one of these latter schools in Chicago, where they were so cautious that they did not teach any sort of history or economics, which was raided in the early part of January, 1920. A general raid under the direction of the federal Department of Justice "ran in" numbers of Chicago suspects on the second, of January, but an enterprising states attorney in Chicago, doubtless craving the political prestige to be thus gained, anticipated the federal action by twenty-four hours and conducted raids on his own account. The immigrants arrested without warrant were thrust into crowded police stations and all other available places of detention. The automobile school was carried off bodily, the teachers, the sixty-four pupils, the books and papers; the latter were considered valuable because the algebraic formulas appeared so incriminating.

One Russian among those arrested on January 1st, 1920, I had known for many years as a member of a Tolstoy society, which I had attended a few times after my visit to Russia in 1896. The society was composed of Russians committed to the theory of non-resistance and anxious to advance the philosophy underlying Tolstoys books. I knew of no group in Chicago whose members I should have considered less dangerous. This man, with twenty-three other prisoners, was thrust into a cell built for eight men. There was no room to sit, even upon the floor, they could only stand closely together, take turns in lying on the benches and in standing by the door where they might exercise by stretching their hands to the top bars. Because they were federal prisoners the police refused to feed them, but by the second day coffee and sandwiches were brought to them by federal officials. But the half-starved Tolstoyan even then would not eat meat nor drink coffee, but waited patiently until his wife found him and could feed him cereals and milk. As a young man he had edited the periodical of a humanitarian society in Russia and it was as a convinced humanitarian that he began to study Tolstoy. Because the grand jury held him for trial under a state charge he could not even be deported if the federal charge were sustained. It was impossible, of course, not to "stand by" old friends such as he and others whom I had known for years, but the experience of securing bail for them; of presiding at a meeting of protest against such violation of constitutional rights; of identification with the vigorous Civil Liberties Union in New York and its Chicago branch, did not add to my respectability in the eyes of my fellow citizens.

And yet the earlier Settlements had believed that the opportunity to live close to the people would enable the residents to know intimately how simple people felt upon fundamental issues and we had hoped that the residents would stand fast to that knowledge in the midst of a social crisis where an interpreter would be valuable. Could not such activity be designated as "settlement work?" It was certainly so regarded by a handful of settlement people in Boston and New York as well as Chicago. There were two contending trends of public opinion at this time which reminded me of the early Settlement days in the United States, one the working mans universal desire for public discussion and the other the employers belief that such discussion per se was dangerous.

In the midst of the world-wide social confusion and distress, there inevitably developed a profound scepticism as to the value of established institutions. The situation in itself afforded a challenge, for men longed to turn from the animosities of war and from the futility of the peace terms to unifying principles, and yet at that very moment any attempt at bold and penetrating discussion was quickly and ruthlessly suppressed as if men had no right to consider together the social conditions surrounding them.

This dread and fear of discussion somewhat accounted for the public sentiment exhibited toward the hundred members of the I. W. W. who were tried in Chicago for sedition. They were held in the Cook County jail for many months awaiting trial. Our jail conditions, which are always bad, were made worse through the inevitable overcrowding resulting from the addition of so many federal prisoners. One of the men died, one became insane, one, a temperamental Irishman, fell into a profound melancholy after he had been obliged to listen throughout the night to the erection of a gallows in the corridor upon which his cell opened where a murderer was "to meet the penalty of the law at dawn." Before the drop fell the prisoners were removed from their cells, but too late to save the mind of one of them. Eleven of the other prisoners contracted tuberculosis and although the federal judge who was hearing the case lowered the bail and released others on their "own recognizance" in order to lessen the fearful risks, the prisoners were then faced with the necessity for earning enough money for lodging and breakfast, before the long day in court began. Fortunately the judge allowed them a dinner and a supper at the expense of the government. Some of us started a "milk fund" for those who were plainly far on the road to tuberculosis and perhaps nothing revealed the state of the public mind more clearly than the fact that while we did collect a fund the people who gave it were in a constant state of panic lest their names become known in connection with this primitive form of charity. The I. W. W. s were not on the whole "pacifists" and I used to regret sometimes that our group should be the one fated to perform this purely humanitarian function which would certainly become associated with sedition in the public mind. We should however logically have escaped all criticism for at that very moment the representatives of "patriotic" societies working in the prison camps of the most backward countries at war, were allowed to separate the tubercular prisoners from their fellows.

The Berger trial came in January of the wretched winter. I had met Victor Berger first when as a young man he had spoken before a society at Hull-House which was being addressed by Benjamin Kidd, the English author of the then very popular book on "Social Evolution." I had seen Mr. Berger occasionally during the period when he was in Washington as a Congressman, and knew that many of the Socialists regarded him as slow because he insisted upon proceeding from one legislative measure to another and had no use for "direct action." And yet here he was indicted with three Chicago men, one a clergyman whom I had known for years, for "conspiring to overthrow the government of the United States."

Later there was the sudden rise of "agents provocateurs" in industrial strikes, and the strikers believed that they were employed at Gary, by the secret service department of the government itself. The stories that were constantly current recalled my bewilderment years ago when the Russian exile Azeff died in Paris. He was considered by one faction as an agent provocateur, by another as a devoted revolutionist. The events of his remarkable life, which were undisputed, might easily support either theory, quite as in a famous English trial for sedition a prisoner, named Watts, had been so used by both sides that the English court itself could not determine his status. It was hard to believe the story that a Russian well known as of the Czars police, had organized twenty-four men in Gary for "direct action," had supplied them freely both with radical literature and with firearms but that fortunately just before the headquarters were raided the strike leaders discovered "the plot," persuaded the Russians that they were being duped by the simple statement that any one who gave them arms in a district under military control, was deliberately putting them in danger of their fives.

So it was perhaps not surprising that the Rus sians became angry and confused and were quite sure that they were being incited and betrayed by government agents. The Russians were even suspicious of help from philanthropists because a man who had been head of the Russian bureau in the Department of Public Information and who had stood by the discredited Sisson letters, had after the discontinuance of the Department been transferred to the Russian Section of the American Red Cross; it was suspected that the Settlements even, although they were furnishing bail, might be in collusion with the Red Cross Society.

I got a certain historic perspective, if not comfort at least enlargement of view, by being able to compare our widespread panic in the United States about Russia to that which prevailed in England during and after the French Revolution. A flood of reactionary pamphlets, similar to those issued by our Security Leagues, had then filled England, teaching contempt of France and her "Liberty," urging confidence in English society as it existed and above all warning of the dangers of any change. Hatred of France, a passionate contentment with things as they were, and a dread of the lower classes, became characteristic of English society. The French Revolution was continually used as a warning, for in it could be seen the inevitable and terrible end of the first steps toward democracy. Even when the panic subsided the temper of society remained unchanged for years, so that in the English horror of any kind of revolution, the struggle of the hand-loom weaver in an agony of adjustment to the changes of machine industry, appeared as a menace against an innocent community.

Was this attitude of the English gentry long since dead, being repeated in our so-called upper classes, especially among people in professional and financial circles? Among them and their families war work opened a new type of activity, more socialized in form than many of them had ever known before, and it also gave an outlet to their higher emotions. In the minds of many good men and women the war itself thus became associated with all that was high and fine and patriotism received the sanction of a dogmatic religion which would brook no heretical difference of opinion. Added to this, of course, were the millions of people throughout the country who were actually in the clutches of those unknown and subhuman forces which may easily destroy the life of mankind. A scholar has said of them, "morally it would seem that these forces are not better but less good than mankind, for man at least loves and pities and tries to understand." Such forces may have been responsible for the mob violence which broke out for a time against alien enemies and so-called "traitors," or it may have been merely the unreason, the superstition, the folly and injustice of the old "law of the herd." There was possibly still another factor in the situation in regard to Russia,–the acid test, a touch of the peculiar bitterness evolved during a strike where property interests are assailed. That typical American, William Allen White, once wrote, "My idea of hell, is a place where every man owns a little property and thinks he is just about to lose it."

Was the challenge which Russia threw down to the present economic system after all the factor most responsible for the unreasoning panic which seemed to hold the nation in its grip, or was it that the war spirit, having been painstakingly evolved by the united press of the civilized world, could not easily be exorcised? The war had made obvious the sheer inability of the world to prevent terror and misery. It had been a great revelation of feebleness, as if weakness, ignorance and overweening nationalism had combined to produce something much more cruel than any calculated cruelty could have been. Was the universal un-happiness which seemed to envelop the United States as well as Europe an inevitable aftermath of war?

So far as we had anticipated any contribution from the non-resistant Russian peasant to the cause of Universal Peace, the events in militarized Russia during the years after the war threw us into black despair. Not only had the Bolshevist leaders produced one of the largest armies in Europe, but disquieting rumors came out of Russia that in order to increase production in their time of need the government had been conscripting men both for industry and transportation. It was quite possible that the Russian revolutionists were making the same mistake in thus forging a new tool for their own use which earlier revolutionists had made when they invented universal military conscription. An example of the failure of trying to cast out the devil by Beezlebub, it had been used as a temporary expedient when the first French revolutionists were fighting "the world," but had gradually become an established thing, and in the end was the chief implement of reaction. It alone has thrown Europe back tremendously, entailing an ever-increasing cost of military establishment and consequent increased withdrawal of manpower from the processes of normal living. The proportion of soldiers in Europe has enormously increased since the middle ages; then out of every thousand men four were soldiers, now out of every thousand men a hundred and twenty to a hundred and fifty are soldiers. These were the figures before the great war.

Even the League of Nations, during the first year of its existence brought little comfort. Inci dent to the irritating and highly individualistic position which the pacifist was forced to assume throughout the war, was the difficulty of combining with his old friends and colleagues in efforts for world organization which seemed so reasonable. Before I went to The Hague in the spring of 1915 I had known something of Mr. Hamilton Holts plan to organize a league whose propaganda should relegate the use of military force to an international police service. It was while we were at The Hague that the great meeting was held in Independence Hall in Philadelphia and the League to Enforce Peace was organized. The program did not attempt to outlaw war but would allow it only under certain carefully defined conditions. It was difficult to resist an invitation to join the new league, and I refused only because its liberal concessions as to the use of warfare seemed to me to add to the dislocation of the times, already so out of joint. Had I yielded to my joining impulse I should certainly have been obliged to resign later. The League to Enforce Peace held a meeting in New York City soon after the United States had entered the war and put forth a program hard to reconcile even with its first statement of principles. But after the armistice had been signed, at a meeting held in Madison, Wisconsin, in the winter of 1919, their clear statement of a League of Nations program brought to their banner many of the doubtful, myself among them.

The later winter and spring of 1919 afforded a wonderful opportunity to talk about the League of Nations. It was all in the making and we, its advocates, had the world before us vui which to illustrate "the hopes of mankind." Among my audiences in the half dozen states in which I lectured there would often be a Pole who rejoiced that after a hundred and fifty years of oppression Poland would be free; an Italian longing impatiently to welcome back Italia Irredenta; a Bohemian exulting that the long struggle of his fellow-countrymen had at last reached success; an Armenian who saw the end of Turkish rule. Conscious at moments that all this portended perhaps too much nationalism, I could only assure myself and an audience absorbed in animated discussion, that such a state of mind was inevitable after war, and would doubtless find its place in the plans being developed in Paris.

I had a sharp reminder in the midst of this halcyon period of hope and expectation that a pacifist could not acceptably talk even of the terms of peace to those who most ardently promoted the war. I had accepted an invitation from a program committee to address one of the long established womans organizations of Chicago upon the League of Nations, only to find that there was a sharp division within the membership as to the propriety of allowing a pacifist to appear before them. The president and the board valiantly stood by the invitation and the address was finally given on the date announced to the half of the club and their friends who were willing to hear. But the incident gave me a curious throw-back into a state of mind I was fast leaving behind me, and although fortunately a day or two later I spoke in Chicago under the direct auspices of the League to Enforce Peace with ex-President Taft presiding, which I afterward learned somewhat restored me among the doubting, I concluded that to the very end pacifists will occasionally realize that they have been permanently crippled in their natural and friendly relations to their fellow citizens.

The League of Nations afforded an opportunity for wide difference of opinion in every group. The Womans Peace Party held its annual meeting in Chicago in the spring of 1920 and found our Branches fairly divided upon the subject. The Boston branch had followed the leadership of the League to Enforce Peace throughout the year and after the Madison meeting others had also, always with the notable exception of the Philadelphia branch, composed largely of clear-sighted Quakers and of two other branches which were more radical. The difference of opinion was limited always as to the existing League and never for a moment did anyone doubt the need for continued effort to bring about an adequate international organization. Some of our members cooperated with the League of Free Nations Association (now the Foreign Policies Association) which had been organized by liberals in order to keep the democratic war aims before the public. Even when peacemaking was going forward at Versailles the association pointed out vulnerable points in the draft at cost of being roundly denounced.

We all believed that the ardor and self sacrifice so characteristic of youth could be enlisted for the vitally energetic role required to inaugurate a new type of international life in the world. We realized that it is only the ardent spirits, the lovers of mankind, who can break down the suspicion and lack of understanding which have so long prevented the changes upon which international good order depend. These men of good will we believed, would at last create a political organization enabling nations to secure without war those high ends which they had vainly although so gallantly sought to obtain upon the battlefield.

CHAPTER X

A FOOD CHALLENGE TO THE LEAGUE OF NATIONS

During the first year of the League of Nations, there were times when we felt that the governments must develope a new set of motives and of habits, certainly a new personnel before they would be able to create a genuine League; that the governmental representatives were fumbling awkwardly at a new task for which their previous training in international relations had absolutely unfitted them.

In a book entitled "International Government" put out by the Fabian Society, its author, Leonard Woolf, demonstrates the super-caution governments traditionally exhibit in regard to all foreign relationships even when under the pressure of great human needs. The illustrations I remember most distinctly were the "International Diplomatic Conferences" following epidemics of cholera in Europe between 1851 and 1892. Five times these Conferences, convened in haste and dread, adjourned without action, largely because each, nation was afraid to delegate any power to an other, lest national sovereignty be impaired. The last European epidemic of cholera broke out in 1892. Even then national prestige and other abstractions dear to the heart of the diplomat confined the quarantine regulations, signed by thirteen states, to ships passing through the Suez Canal, the governments hoping thus to provide a barrier against disease at the point where the streams of pilgrim traffic and Asiatic trading crossed each other. Mr. Woolf points out that if the state had any connection with the people, it was certainly of vital interest that cholera should not be allowed to spread into Europe; but that these genuine human interests were sacrificed to a so-called foreign policy, to "a reputation for finesse and diplomatic adroitness, confined to a tiny circle of government diplomats." In the meantime the pragmatic old world had gone on its way, and because there was developing a new sense of responsibility for public health, scientists and doctors from many nations had become organized into International Associations. In fact there were so many of these, that a "Permanent International Commission of the International Congresses of Medicine" was finally established. Such organizations were doing all sorts of things about cholera, while the governments under which they lived were afraid to act together because each so highly prized its national sovereignty.

Did something of this spirit, still surviving, inevitably tend to inhibit action among the representatives of the nations first collected under the auspices of the League of Nations, and will the League ever be able to depend upon nationalism even multiplied by forty-eight or sixty? Must not the League evoke a human motive transcending and yet embracing all particularist nationalisms, before it can function with validity?

During the first year of the League the popular enthusiasm seemed turned into suspicion, the common man distrusted the League because it was so indifferent to the widespread misery and starvation of the world; because in point of fact it did not end war and was so slow to repair its ravages and to return its remote prisoners; because it so cautiously refused to become the tentative instrument of the longed for new age. Certainly its constitution and early pronouncements were disappointing. During the first months of its existence the League of Nations, apparently ignoring the social conditions of Europe and lacking the incentives which arise from developing economic resources had fallen back upon the political concepts of the 18th century, more abstractly noble than our own perhaps, but frankly borrowed and therefore failing both in fidelity and endurance.

It may be necessary, as has been said, to turn the State and its purposes into an idealistic ab straction before men are willing to fight to the death for it, but it was all the more necessary after the war to come back as quickly as possible to normal motives, to the satisfaction of sintple human needs. It was imperative that there should be a restored balance in human relationships, an avoidance of all the dangers which an overstrained idealism fosters.

This return should have been all the easier because during the world war, literally millions of people had stumbled into a situation where "those great cloud banks of ancestral blindness weighing down upon human nature" seemed to have lifted for a moment and they became conscious of an unexpected sense of relief, as if they had returned to a state of primitive well-being. The old tribal sense of solidarity, of Belonging to the whole, was enormously revived by the war when the strain of a common danger brought the members, not only of one nation but of many nations, into a new realization of solidarity and of a primitive interdependence. In the various armies and later among the civilian populations, two of mens earliest instincts which had existed in age-long companionship became widely operative; the first might be called security from attack, the second security from starvation. Both of them originated in tribal habits and the two motives are still present in some form in all governments.

Throughout the war the first instinct was utilized to its fullest possibility by every device of propaganda when one nation after another was mobilizing for a "purely defensive war."

The second, which might be called security from starvation became the foundation of the great organizations for feeding the armies and for conserving and distributing food supplies among civilian populations.

The suggestion was inevitable that if the first could so dominate the world that ten million young men were ready to spend their lives in its assertion, surely something might be done with the second, also on an international scale, to remake destroyed civilization.

Throughout their period of service in the army, a multitude of young men experienced a primitive relief and healing because they had lost that sense of separateness, which many of them must have cordially detested, the consciousness that they were living differently from the mass of their fellows. As he came home, one returned soldier after another trying to explain why he found it hard to settle back into his previous life, expressed more or less coherently that he missed the sense of comradeship, of belonging to a mass of men. Doubtless the moment of attack, of danger shared in such wise that the life of each man was absolutely dependent upon his comrades courage and steadfastness, were the moments of his highest consciousness of solidarity, but on the other hand he must have caught an expression of it at other times. The soldier knew, that as a mere incident to his great cause, he was being fed and billeted, and the sharing of such fare as the army afforded in simple comradeship, doubtless also gave him a sense of absolute unity. Although the returned men did not talk very freely of their experiences, one gradually confirmed what the newspapers and magazines were then reporting, that the returned soldiers were restless and unhappy. I remember one Sunday afternoon when Hull-House gave a reception to the members of the Hull-House Band, who with their leader had been the nucleus of the I49th Field Artillery Band, serving in France and later in Coblenz, that the young men, obviously glad to be at home, were yet curiously ill-adjusted to the old conditions. They haltingly described the enthusiasm of mass action, the unquestioning comradeship of identical aims which army experiences had brought them.

Throughout the war something of the same enthusiasm had come to be developed in regard to feeding the world. It also became unnatural for an individual to stand outside of the wide-spread effort to avert starvation. He was overwhelmed with a sense of mal-adjustment, of positive wrongdoing if he stressed at that moment the slowly ac quired and substitute virtue of self support, and he even found it difficult to urge the familiar excuse of family obligation which had for so long a time been considered adequate.

This combination of sub-conscious memories and a keen realization of present day needs, overwhelmed many civilians when the grim necessity of feeding millions of soldiers and of relieving the bitter hunger of entire populations in remote countries, was constantly with them. The necessity for rationing stirred that comradeship which is expressed by a common table, and also healed a galling consciousness on the part of many people that they were consuming too much while fellow creatures were starving.

Did soldiers and civilians alike roll off a burden of conscious difference endured from ancestral days, even from simian groups which preceded the human tribes? In their earlier days men so lived that each member of the tribe shared such food and safety as were possible to the whole. Does the sense of burden endured since imply that in the break-up of the tribe and of the patriarchal family, human nature has lost something essential to its happiness? The great religious teachers may have attempted to restore it when they have preached the doctrine of sharing the life of the meanest and of renouncing all until the man at the bottom is fed.

For the moment, at least, two of the old tribal virtues were in the ascendancy and the fascination of exercising them was expressed equally by the Red Cross worker who felt as if she "had never really lived before" and actually dreaded to resume her pre-war existence, and the returned soldier who had discovered such a genuine comradeship that he pronounced the old college esprit de corps tame by contrast.

Human nature, in spite of its marvelous adaptability, has never quite fitted its back to the moral strain involved in the knowledge that fellow creatures are starving. In one generation this strain subsides to an uneasy sense of moral discomfort, in another it rises to a consciousness of moral obliquity; it has lain at the basis of many religious communities and social experiments, and in our own generation is finding extreme expression in governmental communism. In the face of the widespread famine, following the devastation of war, it was inevitable that those political and social institutions which prevented the adequate production and distribution of food should be sharply challenged. Hungry men asked themselves why such a situation should exist, when the world was capable of producing a sufficient food supply. We forgot not only that the world itself had been profoundly modified by the war, but that the minds which appraise it had also been repolarized as they were forced to look at life from the point of view of primitive human needs.

To different groups of men all over the world therefore the time had apparently now come to make certain that all human creatures should be insured against death by starvation. They did not so much follow the religious command as a primitive instinct to feed the hungry, although in a sense these economic experiments of our own time are but the counterpart of the religious experiments of another age.

During the first months of so-called peace when everywhere in Europe the advantage shifted from the industrial town to the food-producing country, it seemed reasonable to believe that the existing governments, from their war experiences in the increased production and distribution of foods, might use the training of war to meet the great underlying demand reasonably and quickly. In point of fact, during the first year after the war, five European cabinets fell, due largely to the grinding poverty resulting from the prolonged war. Two of these governments fell avowedly over the sudden rise in the price of bread which had been subsidized and sold at a fraction of its cost.

The demand for food was recognized and acknowledged as in a great measure valid, but it was being met in piecemeal fashion while a much needed change in the worlds affairs threatened to occur under the leadership of men driven desperate by hunger. In point of fact, the demand could only be met adequately if the situation were treated on an international basis, the nations working together whole-heartedly to fulfill a world obligation. If from the very first the League of Nations could have performed an act of faith which marked it at once as the instrument of a new era, if it had evinced the daring to meet new demands which could have been met in no other way, then, and then only would it have become the necessary instrumentality to carry on the enlarged life of the world and would have been recognized as indispensable.

Certain it is that for two years after the war the League of Nations was in dire need of an overmastering motive forcing it to function and to justify itself to an expectant world, even to endear itself to its own adherents. As the war had demonstrated how much stronger is the instinct of self-defense than any motives for a purely private good, so one dreamed that the period of commercial depression following the war might make clear the necessity for an appeal to the much wider and profounder instinct responsible for conserving human life.

In the first years after the cessation of the great war there was all over the world a sense of loss in motive power, the consciousness that there was no driving force equal to that furnished by the heroism and self-sacrifice so lately demanded. The great principles embodied in the League of Nations, rational and even appealing though they were, grew vague in mens minds because it was difficult to make them objective. There seemed no motive for their immediate utilization. But what could have afforded a more primitive, genuine and abiding motive tharffeeding the peoples of the earth on an international scale, utilizing all the courage and self-sacrifice evolved by the war. All that international administration which performed such miracles of production in the prosecution of the war was defined by the British Labor Party at its annual conference in 1919 as "a world-government actually in being which should be made the beginnings of a constructive international society."

The British Labor Party, therefore, recommended three concrete measures apart from the revision of the Peace Treaty, as follows: 1. A complete raising of the blockade EVERYWHERE, in PRACTICE as well as IN NAME.

2. Granting CREDITS to enemy and to liberated countries alike, to enable them to obtain food and raw materials sufficient to put them in a position where they can begin to help themselves.

3. Measures for the special relief of children EVERYWHERE, without regard to the political allegiance of their parents.

How simple and adequate these three recommendations were and yet how far-reaching in their consequences! They would first of all have compelled the promoters of the League to drop the 18th century phrases in which diplomatic intercourse is conducted, atid to substitute plain economic terms fitted to the matter in hand. Such a course would have forced them to an immediate discussion of credit for reconstruction purposes, the need of an internationally guaranteed loan, the function of a recognized international Economic Council for the control of food stuffs and raw material, the world-wide fuel shortage, the effect of mal-nutrition on powers of production, the irreparable results of "hunger oedema."

The situation presented material for that genuine and straightforward statesmanship which was absolutely essential to the feeding of Europes hungry children. An atmosphere of discussion and fiery knowledge of current conditions as revealed by war, once established, the promoters of the League would experience "the zeal, the tingle, the excitement of reality" which the League so sadly lacked. The promoters of the League had unhappily assumed that the rights of the League are anterior to and independent of its functioning, forgetting that men are instinctively wary in accepting at their face value high-sounding claims which cannot justify themselves by achievement, and that in the long run "authority must go with function." They also ignored the fact that the stimuli they were utilizing failed to evoke an adequate response for this advanced form, of human effort.

The adherents of the League often spoke as if they were defending a too radical document whereas it probably failed to command widespread confidence because it was not radical enough, because it clung in practice at least to the old self-convicted diplomacy. But the common man in a score of nations could not forget that this diplomacy had failed to avert a war responsible for the death of ten million soldiers, as many more civilians, with the loss of an unestimated amount of civilization goods, and that all the revolutionary governments since the world began could not be charged with a more ghastly toll of human life and with a heavier destruction of property.

During those months of uncertainty and anxiety the governments responsible for the devastations of a world war were unaccountably timid in undertaking restoration on the same scale, and persistently hesitated to discharge their obvious obligations.

It was self-evident that if the League refused to become the instrument of a new order, all the difficult problems resulting, at least in their present acute form, from a world war, would be turned over to those who must advocate revolution in order to obtain the satisfaction of acknowledged human needs. It was deplorable that this great human experiment should be entrusted solely to those who must appeal to the desperate need of the hungry to feed themselves, whereas this demand, in its various aspects seemed to afford a great controlling motive in the world at the present moment, as political democracy, as religious freedom, had moved the world at other times.

There were many occasions during the first year of the Leagues existence when the necessity for such action was fairly forced upon its attention.

At Paris, in May, 1920, when the association of Red Cross societies was organized, committing itself to the fight against tuberculosis, to a well considered program of Child Welfare and to other humanitarian measures for devastated Europe, a letter was received from Mr. Balfour on behalf of the League of Nations. He made an eloquent appeal for succor against the disease afflicting the war worn and underfed populations of central and western Europe. The Association of Red Cross Societies replied that it was the starving man who most readily contracts ajnd spreads disease, and that only if the Allied governments supplied loans to these unhappy nations could food and medical supplies be secured; that according to a report made recently to them, "There were found everywhere never-ending vicious circles of political paradox and

economic complication, with consequent paralysis of national life and industry. "
This diagnosis gave a clue to the situation, indicating that the League of Nations must
abandon its political treatment of war worn Europe and consider the starving people
as its own concrete problem. The recognition of this obvious moral obligation and
a generous attempt to fulfill it, even to the point if need be of losing the life of the
League, might have resulted in the one line of action which would most quickly have
saved it. If the coal, the iron, the oil and above all the grain had been distributed under
international control from the first day of the armistice, Europe might have escaped
the starvation from which she suffered for months. The League could actually have
laid the foundations of that type of government towards which the world is striving
and in which it is so persistently experimenting.

The great stumbling block in the way of an earlier realization of this dream of a
League of Peace has been what is the crux of its actual survival now, the difficulty in
interpreting it to the understanding of the common man, grounding it in his affections,
appealing to his love for human kind. To such men, who after all compose the bulk
of the citizens in every nation participating in the League, the abstract politics of it
make little appeal, although they would gladly contribute their utmost to feed the
starving. Two and a half million French trade unionists regularly taxed themselves
for the children of Austria; the British Labor Party insisted that the British foreign
policy should rest "upon a humane basis, really caring for all mankind, including
colored men, women and children;" and the American Federation of Labor declared
its readiness to "give a mighty service in a common effort for all human kind." So far
as the working man in any country expressed himself, it was always in this direction.
Perhaps it was unfair to expect so much in the first years after the establishment of the
League, when it was crippled by the uncertain attitude of the United States. But all the
more its friends longed to find, or rather to release, some basic human emotion which
should bring together men of good-will on both sides of the Atlantic. A close observer
of the Paris Peace Conference had said that it was an extraordinary fact that starving
Europe was the one subject upon which it had been impossible to engage the attention
of the "big four" throughout their long deliberations. Yet in the popular discussions
of the functions of the League the feeding of the people appeared constantly like an
unhappy ghost that would not down.

While the first year of the League held much that was discouraging for its advocates,
the first meeting of the Assembly convened in Geneva in November, 1920, resolved
certain doubts and removed certain inhibitions from the minds of many of us. The
Assembly demonstrated that after all it was possible for representatives from the
nations of the earth to get together in order to discuss openly, freely, kindly for the
most part, and even unselfishly, the genuine needs of the world. In spite of the special
position of the Great Powers, this meeting of the Assembly had so increased the moral
prestige of the League of Nations that it was reasonable to believe that an articulate
world-opinion would eventually remove the treaty entanglements which threatened
to frustrate the very objects of the League. The small nations, represented by such
men as Nansen and Branting, not by insistence on the doctrine of the sovereignty
and equality of states, but through sheer devotion to world interests, were making the
League effective and certainly more democratic. Perhaps these representatives were

acting, not only from their own preferences or even convictions, but also from the social impact upon them, from the momentum of life itself.

In many ways the first meeting of the Assembly had been like the beginning of a new era, and it seemed possible that the public discussion, the good-will, and the international concern, must eventually affect the European situation.

During the following year the League of Nations itself inaugurated and carried out many measures which might be designated as purely humanitarian. In the "Report to the Second Assembly of the League on the Work of the Council and on the measures taken to execute the decisions of the First Assembly" in Geneva on September 7th, 1921, under the heading of General International Activities of the League was the following list:

C. I. The repatriation of prisoners.

C. 2. The relief of Russian refugees.

C. 3. General relief work in Europe.

C. 4. The protection of children.

Under "the measures taken in execution of the resolutions and recommendation of the Assembly," in addition to the reports of the Health Organizations, were others such as the campaign against typhus in Eastern Europe, and the relief of children in countries affected by the war. From one aspect these activities were all in the nature of repairing the ravages of the Great War, but it was obvious that further undertakings of the League must be greatly influenced and directed by these early human efforts.

The International Labor Organization, from the first such a hopeful part of the League of Nations, had just concluded as we reached Geneva in August 1921, a conference upon immigration and possible protective measures which the present situation demanded. For many years I had been a Vice President of the American Branch of the International Association for Labour Legislation and had learned only too well how difficult it was to secure equality of conditions for the labor of immigrants. The most touching interviews I have ever had upon the League of Nations had been with simple immigrants in the neighborhood of Hull-House, who had many times expressed the hope that the League might afford some adequate protection to migratory workmen, to the Italian for instance, who begins harvesting the crops south of the equator and, following the ripening grain through one country after another, finally arrives in Manitoba or the Dakotas. He often finds himself far from consular offices, encounters untold difficulties, sometimes falling into absolute peonage.

It was interesting to have the International Labour Organization declare in its report that the two great "peoples" who had first recognized the large part the Office might play in conciliation and protection were (1) the Shipowners and Seamen, as had been shown by the conference at Genoa, and (2) "the immense people of immigrants, the masses who, uprooted from their homelands, ask for some measure of security and protection applicable to all countries and supervised by an international authority."

There was something very reassuring in this plain dealing with homely problems with which I had been so long familiar. I had always been ready to admit that "the solemn declaration of principles which serve to express the unanimity of the aspirations of humanity have immense value," but this was something more concrete, as were other efforts on the part of the Office to defend labor throughout the world and to push forward adequate legislation on their behalf.

In the reaction, which had gained such headway during the two years of peace, against the generous hopes for a better world order the International Labour Organization as well as the League of Nations was encountering all the hazards of a great social experiment. We could but hope that the former might gain some backing from the international congress, to be held in October, 1921, of working women, bringing their enthusiasms and achievements from all parts of the world.

The food challenge was put up fairly and squarely to the Second meeting of the Assembly of the League of Nations by the Russian famine due to the prolonged drought of 1921. A meeting to consider the emergency had been called in Geneva in August, under the joint auspices of the International Red Cross and the League of Red Cross Societies. We were able to send a representative to it from our Womans International League almost directly from our Third International Congress in Vienna. There was every possibility for using the dire situation in Russia for political ends, both by the Soviet Government and by those offering relief. On the other hand, there was a chance that these millions of starving people, simply because their need was so colossal that any other agency would be pitifully inadequate, would receive help directly from many governments, united in a mission of good-will. It was a situation which might turn mens minds from war and a disastrous peace to great and simple human issues; in such an enterprise the governments would "realize the failure of national coercive power for indispensable ends like food for the people," they would come to a cooperation born of the failure of force.

Dr. Fridjof Nansen, appointed high commissioner at the Red Cross meeting in August, after a survey of the Russian Famine regions returned to Geneva for the opening of the Assembly on September 5th, in which he represented Norway, with a preliminary report of Russian conditions. He made a noble plea, which I was privileged to hear, that the delegates in the Assembly should urge upon their governments national loans which should be adequate to furnish the gigantic sums necessary to relieve twenty-five million starving people.

As I listened to this touching appeal on behalf of the helpless I was stirred to a new hope for the League. I believed that, although it may take years to popularize the principles of international cooperation, it is fair to remember that citizens of all the nations have already received much instruction in world-religions. To feed the hungry on an international scale might result not only in saving the League but in that world-wide religious revival which, in spite of many predictions during and since the war, had as yet failed to come. It was evident in the meeting of the Assembly that Dr. Nansen had the powerful backing of the British delegates as well as others, and it was therefore a matter for unexpected as well as for bitter disappointment when his plea was finally denied. This denial was made at the very moment when the Russian peasants, in the center of the famine district, although starving, piously abstained from eating the seed grain and said to each other as they scattered it over the ground for their crop of winter wheat; "We must sow the grain although we shall not live to see it sprout."

Did the delegates in the Assembly still retain the national grievances and animosities so paramount when the League of Nations was organized in Paris or were they dominated by a fear and hatred of Bolshevism and a panic lest the feeding of Russian peasants should in some wise aid the purposes of Lenines government? Again I reflected that these men of the Assembly, as other men, were still held apart by suspicion and fear, which could only be quenched by motives lying deeper than those responsible for their sense of estrangement.

This sense of human solidarity for the moment seemed most readily obtained by men leading lives of humble toil and self-denial, as if they might teach a war-weary world that the religious revival which alone would be able to fuse together the hostile nations, could never occur unless there were first a conviction of sin, a repentance for the war itself! As long as men contended that the war was "necessary" or "inevitable" the world could not hope for a manifestation of that religious impulse which feeds men solely and only because they are hungry.

A genuine Society of Nations may finally be evolved by millions of earths humblest toilers, whose lives are consumed in securing the daily needs of existence for themselves and their families. They go stumbling towards the light of better international relations, driven forward because "Man is constantly seeking a new and finer adjustment between his inner emotional demands and the practical arrangemehts of the world in which he lives."

CHAPTER XL IN EUROPE AFTER TWO YEARS OF PEACE

Our Third International Congress was held at Vienna in July, 1921, almost exactly two years after the Peace of Versailles had been signed. This third Congress was of necessity unlike the other two in tension and temper and in some respects more difficult. At the first one, held at The Hague in 1915, women came together not only to make a protest against war but to present suggestions for consideration at the final Peace Conference, which, as no one could forsee the duration of the war, everyone then believed might be held within a few months. The second Congress was held in Zurich in 1919 and, while there was open disappointment over the terms of the Treaty, the Peace Commission was still sitting in Paris, and it was believed not only that the terms would be modified but that the constitution of the League of Nations would be developed and ennobled. Both of the earlier Congresses therefore were hopeful in the sense that the better international relationships which were widely supposed to be attained at the end of the war, were still in the making. The third Congress was convened in Vienna, which, as we realized, had suffered bitterly both from the war and the terms of Peace. The women from the thirty countries represented there had been sorely disillusioned by their experiences during the two years of peace, and each group inevitably reflected something of the hopelessness and confusion which had characterized Europe since the war. Nevertheless these groups of women were united in one thing. They all alike had come to realize that every crusade, every beginning of social change, must start from small numbers of people convinced of the righteousness of a cause; that the coming together of convinced groups is a natural process of growth. Our groups had come together in Vienna hoping to receive the momentum and sense of validity which results from encountering like-minded people from other countries and to tell each other how far we had been able to translate conviction into action. The desire to perform the office of reconciliation, to bring something of healing to the confused situation, and to give an impulse towards more normal relations between differing nations, races and classes, was evident from the first meeting of the Congress. This latter was registered in the various proposals, such as that founded upon experiences of the last year, that peace missions composed of women of differ ent nations should visit the borders still in a disturbed condition and also the countries in which war had never really ceased.

There was constant evidence that the food blockade maintained in some instances long after the war, had outraged a primitive instinct of women almost more than the military operations themselves had done. Women had felt an actual repulsion against the slow starvation, the general lowering in the health and resistance of entire pop- ulations, the anguish of the millions of mothers who could not fulfill the primitive obligation of keeping their children alive. There was a certain sternness of attitude con- cerning political conditions which so wretchedly affected womans age-long business of nurturing children, as if women had realized as never before what war means.

In spite of the pressure of these questions the first public meeting was a memorial to Baroness von Suttner, whose remarkable book "Ground Arms" had had a wide reading rivalled by no other book perhaps, save "Uncle Toms Cabin." The book had been an important factor in the history of European militarism and its Austrian author had been honored in many lands.

The first business sessions of the Congress concerned themselves with the age-old question of education. An extraordinarily illuminating di vergence developed from the conflicting experience of Germany and Austria; speakers from Germany attributed Germanys readiness for war largely to their own state monopoly of education, which had, for fifty years, consistently fostered militarism. Austrian women, on the contrary, in whose country one of the most precious gains of the revolution is the transfer of the schools from ecclesiastical authority to the control of the secularized state, overflowed with untried confidence in their newly acquired power as citizens. Among them was the woman member of the National Department of Education. This discussion was but one of many indications that the delegates represented nations in various stages of political and social development. At moments we seemed to be discussing the same question from the experiences of its decadent end and its promising beginnings, as if the delegates to the Congress represented the point of view both of the university and of the kindergarten. Partly Because the meeting was held in Vienna, and partly because the International Secretary, Miss Balch, had recently travelled in the Balkan States in the interests of our League, a large number of women came from the immediate territory. Miss Balch, years before when collecting material for her book entitled "Our Slavic Fellowcitizens," had made many friends in Southeastern Europe and because they appreciated the unusual insight with which she had portrayed the situation then, they were ready to trust her again. Some of them, from Greece, Bulgaria, Poland and the Ukraine, represented organized branches of the League. Other groups were from "minorities" in the newly annexed territories, who frankly came in search of aid, hoping to gain some international recognition and support from even so small and unofficial a Congress as our own. There was an interesting group from Croatia, whose reports of the pacifist movement among the Croatian peasants were most impressive, especially one given by the daughter of Radek, the leader of the movement he believed destined to reassert the non-resistant character of the Slav. The Saxon group from the part of Transylvania which had lately been given over to Roumania, reported religious difficulties; the relation between Bulgaria and Greece with reference to the transfer of nationalities under the League of Nations plan was set forth by women from both countries. At the evening meeting these various minorities, fourteen in all, stated their own cases and resolutions were presented only after the substance had been agreed upon by representatives of both nations involved. Thus the Polish and German women agreed on a resolution about Upper Silesia, the English and Irish delegates on the Irish question. Touching ad dresses were made for the Armenians, for the Zionists and, by a colored woman from the United States, on behalf of her own people who were not nominally a minority, although they often suffered as such. This evenings program cohered with the discussion: "How can a population, feeling that it is suffering from injustice, strive to right its wrongs without violence?" There was a very sympathetic report of the Ghandi movement given by Miss Picton Turberville, who had lived in India and who preached the following Sunday for our Congress in the English Church in Vienna. We were also told of a remarkable group centering about Bilthoven in Holland, with some detail as to how Norway and Sweden had accomplished their separation without bloodshed, and of the earlier non-resistant phases of the Sinn Fein movement. Nearly every country represented by a delegation brought some report of the "non-military movement," in which large or smaller numbers of their fellow-citizens had pledged themselves to take no part in war or in its preparation. Four of our own branches, all of them in countries recently at war, had made this promise of non-cooperation in war a test of membership in the national organizations.

This was part of the revolt against the precautions the governments of Europe were everywhere taking in regard to pacifist teaching." Even neutral Switzerland had passed a measure in its Assembly, which was still however to be submitted to a referendum of the people, that anyone teaching a man of military age in such wise as to lessen his enthusiasm for military service should be liable to three years imprisonment. A well-known theological professor in a Swiss University had resigned on the ground that he could no longer expound the doctrines of the New Testament to the men in his classes. Holland was considering similar regulations, and even in those countries where universal military service was forbidden by the terms of the Peace Treaty, as in Hungary and Bavaria, the almost military rule temporarily established in both of them made any form of peace propaganda extremely dangerous. It was as if the war spirit itself had to be sustained by force, as if its own adherents were afraid of any open discussion of its moral bases and social implications. The military pairties seemed more and more to confine their appeal to "the sense of security" and to use the old "fear of attack" motives.

We had a brilliant report on what our organization had been able to do from our Geneva headquarters in connection with the League of Nations. This report was accepted with approval authorizing a continuance of the same activity, but there was as usual a minority of the delegates who distrusted the imperialistic designs of the larger nations, and yet another group who believed that, while a useful agency for many international activities, the League of Nations could never secure peace until the most basic changes were made both in its purpose and personnel. So we once more took no official action regarding the League of Nations, but went on in a modus vi-vendi, allowing the greatest latitude to our International Headquarters and to our National Branches. On the other hand, the Dutch Section brought a carefully prepared indictment of the construction of the League and urged work for changes in the Treaty as a paramount obligation. The few Communists who were delegates to the Congress–the word used in Europe in a some what technical sense to designate the members of the Left in the Socialist Party–were perhaps the most discouraged people there, because their movement in Russia and elsewhere had become so absolutely militaristic. Holding to their pacifist principles had cost them their standing in their own party. Although they may have "come high" to us so far as public opinion was concerned, no people in the world at that moment so needed the companionship which pacifist groups might give them: in the eyes of the bourgeoisie themselves, no one could put pacifism into practice more beneficially for all Europe. These few Communist delegates were for the most part reasonable, but all of them were profoundly discouraged.

The resolution which excited the most comment in the press, and which apparently aroused that white heat of interest attaching to any discussion, however remote, of property privileges, was introduced by a group who felt that, as we constantly urged the revolutionist to pacific methods and denounced violence between the classes as we did between the nations, we should logically "work to awaken and strengthen among members of the possessing classes the earnest wish to transform the economic system in the direction of social justice." The methods suggested in the resolution and voted upon subsequently were "by means of taxation, death duties and reform in land laws," all of them in operation in many of the countries represented in the Congress. The momentary sense of panic aroused by this reasonable discussion, was an indication of that unrestrained fear of Bolshevism encountered everywhere in Europe. It was hard to determine whether it was the idea itself which was so terrifying or the army of the Russian Bolshevists threatening to enforce a theory regardless of "consent." At any rate, a European public found it hard to believe that anything even remotely connected with private property could be discussed upon its merits and was convinced that the subject must have been introduced either by agents provocateurs, or by propagandists paid with Russian money. The war propaganda had demonstrated to the world how possible it is "to put over" an opinion if enough ability and money are expended and Europeans thought they had learned to detect it. We undoubtedly felt for an instant that icy breath of fear blowing through Europe from the mysterious steppes of Russia.

Throughout the Congress we were conscious that peace theories turned into action won the complete admiration of the delegates as nothing else did. This was instanced when the Congress was eloquently addressed by a Belgian delegate, Madame Lucie Dejardin. She had been carried into Germany in January, 1915, and worked there in one camp after another, until, developing tuberculosis, she was invalided to Switzerland in July, 1918. Upon her return to Belgium she had organized an association of those who had been imprisoned in Germany, civilians as well as returned Belgian soldiers, that they might feed German and Austrian children. She reported to the Congress that the association had received 2,000 of these children as guests in Belgium. She gave this information incidentally in the speech she was making to thank the various nations represented there for what they had done for the relief of her own compatriots., This Belgian woman was typical of many women who had touched bottom as it were in the valley of human sorrow and had found a spring of healing there.

We found everywhere in Austria the impossible situation so often described as "a combination of concrete obstacles with psychological deterrents, all operating through a degraded and constantly falling currency." The effective ability in labor, business, domestic and intellectual life, had all sustained heavy damages through the war, through the blockade, through the Peace terms and through the post-war economic policy. All the people had been piteously reduced by privations. The professional and artistic people had gradually lowered their standard of living to that below the health line. In addition the insolvency threatened to destroy the collective resources of culture and education: everywhere we were told that there was no money to buy books and periodicals for long-established libraries, that schools were closing, that orchestras were forced to disband. The students feeding in various Universities which we visited both in Austria and in the neighboring states seemed somewhat like the students commons we are all accustomed to see in endowed institutions, but it was a distinct shock to be invited to a luncheon with distinguished professors who were also eating subsidized ra tions. So many of these men were accepting posts elsewhere that Austria was threatened with the loss of her most brilliant scholars.

There were many forms of relief throughout the city of Vienna. We naturally saw most of the American Relief Administration established by Mr. Hoover, and of the Friends Service Committee, with which several Hull-House residents were identified. The head of the latter, Dr. Hilda Clark, from England, had been in Vienna during the armistice and had brought back an early report of the children in whose behalf she had since organized a large unit of relief. This fed thousands of children below school age as well as groups of the aged in all classes of society who had poignantly felt that they had no right to live at the expense of food for the young. The Quakers were much beloved everywhere, as were other groups from all of the neutral, and many of the belligerent countries in Europe who were coming to the rescue of the Viennese children, taking them out of Austria even as far as northern Sweden that they might have better care and food. They were alleviating the situation in hundreds of ways although in spite of these united efforts only 21 children out of a 100 were as yet approximately normal. It was as if the world, aghast at what had happened to these children, was putting into the situation all the inventiveness and resource that human compassion could devise. Out of it was developing what might prove to be a new and higher standard for the care of children, one which might become a norm for the whole world to use. Dr. Pirquets clinic, with its carefully devised tests for nutrition and growth, the thousands of school children fed by the A. R. A., with the attendant medical examination, the huge barracks everywhere turned into sanatoria for tubercular and convalescent children, all suggested a higher standard of public care than that obtained in any other city. Even the educational requirements seemed pushed forward by the dire experience; I have never heard children sing more beautifully, nor seen them dance with more grace and charm, than those Austrian children celebrating the 4th of July in the American Milk Relief Barracks, while a new possibility in childrens drawing was being set by Professor Cizek. That this new standard would be Viennas gift to the world in exchange for what the world was trying to do for her children was perhaps the one ray of light in what could but be a dark future. In talks with the Austrian Food Administrator and with the Minister of Agriculture; in lectures given to the Congress by the economist, Professor Hertz, and by the Minister of Public Welfare, there was always the inevitable conclusion, although stated with restraint, that the Peace Treaty had placed Austria in an impossible position.

Perhaps it was because the Viennese were pleased to have their city selected as the seat for an international Congress, that they extended us such boundless hospitality. The Congress was received in the offices of the Foreign Minister, by the President of the Republic and the entire diplomatic corps; in the City Hall by the Mayor and the heads of the Administrative Departments; we were entertained by various musical societies, and everything possible was done to demonstrate that an old cultivated city was making welcome members of an international body. This public hospitality, in which women officials took such a natural and reasonable place, was in marked contrast to my former experience in Austria. In 1913 I had attended the Suffrage Meeting in Vienna presided over by the mother of the present President of the Austrian Republic. At that time the Austrian women were prohibited by law from belonging to any organization with a political aim. I returned eight years later, as I said at a public reception in the City Hall, to find full suffrage extended to all women over twenty-one years old, with eleven women sitting in the lower House of Parliament, four in the Upper House, and twenty-three as members of the City Council. In the face of these rapid changes, who would venture to say that peace or any other unpopular cause, was hopeless. Even a new basis for bread peace seemed not so remote when the large audience, containing many Austrian officials, listened with profound interest to a Frenchwoman, Mile. Melin, who, although her devastated home was not yet rebuilt, held war itself as an institution responsible for the wretched world in which we are all living. She spoke superbly then, as she did once more, the Thursday following the Congress, when again in the City Hall she addressed an audience of wounded soldiers who applauded to the echo this Frenchwoman telling them there could be no victor in modern warfare.

At the end of the Congress an International Summer School was held in the charming old town of Salzburg. Students came from twenty different countries, the largest number from Great Britain. The lectures, in English, French and German, were delivered by men and women from a dozen nations on the psychological, the economic, the historic and biological causes of war. They were provocative of thought and discussion in the class room itself and later among the eager students, who constantly arranged special meetings, one every morning at seven oclock on a mountain top. Again the impression we received, as in Vienna at the Congress itself, was one of vitality and energy, as of a fresh growth pushing through old traditions. The Movement of Youth represented by many of the German students was making a fresh demand upon life for reality and simplicity which was in strange contrast to a contention made by one of the lecturers on science when he compared "the will to possess with the will to live," showing, with a wealth of illustration, that the former was apparently becoming stronger than the latter. A discussion at the Vienna Congress brought support to this theory, contending that it was possible for people to oppose the socialization of wealth while at the same time they advocated the conscription of life. Delegates from two of the war-stricken countries, one group from each side of the recent war, were quite certain that future wars might be prevented if at the very moment that war was declared an automatic conscription of property could take place similar to the conscription of young men. And yet the very ardor and vitality of our younger delegates, led by the able and spirited young secretary of the German section, Gertrude Baer, constantly challenged any theory which could balance property in the pan of the scales against human life.

Was it not rather that youth, "fashioning the glory of the years to be," was transforming property! Certainly we felt everywhere in the midst of the political depression both urge and zest in the efforts of one country after another to restore the land to the people, or at least to divide up the huge estates into smaller holdings. In Hungary, for instance, Barnar Berga, the Minister of Agriculture under the Karoly Government, had been succeeded by a peasant named Sabot, who in the midst of the reaction was putting through radical land reforms of which he talked to us with enthusiasm.

The Czecho-Slovak Government was dividing the estates in the annexed territories among the returned Russian legionaries and other soldiers, and their projected reforms reached much further. Everywhere there was acquiescence if not a "consent" to the housing arrangements which practically all the. cities had made; conservative women told us with a certain pride of what they had done to conform to the municipal regulations in making room for other families within their houses, and that it was "not so bad." Sometimes this sympathetic report and the universal concern for the starving children, gave one hope that this impulse to care for the victims of the war might become as wide-spread as its devastating misery, expressing itself not only through the care of children but in many other ways, such as the governmental subsidy to the bread supply which was still regularly made in Austria. Would this impulse gradually subside into a "suppressed desire," forming the basis of futile and disturbing social unrest, would it be seized by the doctrinaires who were already trading so largely upon the normal human impulses exaggerated by war, or would it finally be captured by the friends of mankind? Could not this impulse to nurture the wretched be canalized and directed by enlarged governmental agencies, and was not that the problem before the statesmen of Europe?

The conditions in Southeastern Europe as we met them that hot summer of 1921 might well challenge the highest statesmanship. We saw much of starvation and we continually heard of the appalling misery in all of the broad belt lying between the Baltic and the Black Seas, to say nothing of Russia to the east and Armenia to the south. Even those food resources which were produced in Europe itself and should have been available for instant use, were prevented from satisfying the desperate human needs by "jealous and cruel tariff regulations surrounding each nation like the barbed wire entanglements around a concentration camp." A covert war was being carried on by the use of import duties and protective tariffs to such an extent that we felt as if economic hostility, having been legitimatized by the food blockades of the war, was of necessity being sanctioned by the very commissions which were the outgrowth of the Peace Conference itself. We saw that the smaller states, desperately protecting themselves against each other, but imitated the great Allies with their protectionist policies, with their colonial monopolies and preferences.

This economic war may have been inevitable, especially between successsion States of the former Austrian Empire with their inherited oppressions and grievances. Yet we longed for a Customs Union, a Pax Economica for these new nations, who failed to see that "the price of nationality is a workable internationalism, otherwise it is doomed so far as the smaller states are concerned."

We arrived in Europe in the midst of the prolonged discussion as to the amount of the "reparations" to be paid by Germany. This discussion by the Supreme Council had focussed more powerfully than ever before the antagonism between two conceptions of international trade; one, that widest form of cooperation which would afford the greatest yield of wealth to the entire world; the other, that conflict of activities and interests by which the members of one nation may, through governmental action, benefit themselves at the cost of the members of other nations. The latter doctrine was of course openly applied to the enemy nations, but naturally it could not be confined to them.

We had established our own bakery in Vienna, that delegates might not "eat bread away from the Viennese," and special food arrangements had been made for our students in Salzburg. Yet there was always the shadow of the insufficient food supply. In the region of Salzburg, children were being fed by the A. R. A. throughout a countryside which ordinarily exported milk products. The under-nourished students who filled the streets of the music-loving city during the Mozart week, which was celebrated by daily concerts during the term of our School, were a silent reproach to ones prosperity. We became impatient with the long-delayed action on the report of the Economic Commission sent to study Austrias needs, and felt that food and raw materials must come quickly if Austria were to be saved from an economic and moral collapse.

The situation as we saw it seemed to bear out completely Norman Angells theory of the futility of war. As he stated in "The Fruits of Victory," published at that time; "The continent as a whole has the same soil and natural resources and technical knowledge as when it fed its population but there is suffering and want on every hand. War psychology is fatal to social living. The ideas which produce war–the fears out of which it grows and the passions which it feeds–produce a state of mind that ultimately renders impossible the cooperation by which alone wealth can be produced and life maintained."

The situation therefore resolves itself into the dominance of ideas, into the temper of mind which makes war possible. Even the pro-war newspapers were then recognizing it. A leading journal, a consistent apologist for the great war, had written: "Europe will never recover composure and peace, nor can an acceptable and workable compromise be achieved, until the consequences of the method of coercion are understood and the method itself abandoned in the interest of a method of consent."

And so we came back to what our own organization was trying to do, to substitute consent for coercion, a will to peace for a belief in war. Like all educational efforts, from the preaching in churches to the teaching in schools, at moments it must seem ineffectual and vague, but after all the activities of life can be changed in no other way than by changing the current ideas upon which it is conducted.

The members of the Womans International League for Peace and Freedom had certainly learned from their experience during the war that widely accepted ideas can be both dominating and all powerful. But we still believed it possible to modify, to direct and ultimately to change current ideas, not only through discussion and careful pre sentation of facts, but also through the propaganda of the deed.

In accord with the latter, one German section, after our Congress in Vienna had sent a group of women into Upper Silesia, which at that time was filled with ardent nationalists both for Germany and Poland, each hotly presenting the claims of his own side. The group of women entered the contested territory, not to promote either national claim but to counsel confidence in the good intentions of those making the final decision; to preach that freedom of exchange in coal or other commodities is more basic to economic life than any detail of political boundaries; to abate the hyper-nationalistic feeling which was responsible for actual warfare between the non-contending peoples.

In fact it seemed to me during that summer as I visited one National Section after another, that all of our members in their daily walk and conversation had been bearing unequivocal testimony against war and its methods. This impression was equally vivid at the public meeting at Budapest where Vilma Glucklich presided sitting next to a police officer; as it was later at a meeting in London where Mrs. Swanwick, occupying the platform with a distinguished economist, brilliantly inaugurated a frank discussion of post-war conditions in Europe.

The International Office of our League was established in a charming old house in Geneva. It seemed to me that June day of 1921, as I went through its rose-filled garden, that we might be profoundly grateful if our organization was able in any degree to push forward the purposes of the League of Nations and to make its meaning clearer. Catherine Marshall of England, our referent on the League, had prepared a full and encouraging report for the Vienna Congress of what our office had been able to do in that direction. Personal friends and other members of the Secretariat had taken great pains to have us see and understand the working of that new-found device, with its elaborated Sections and Standing Committees. An ample building was filled with men and a few women, committed to study questions in the interest of many nations, not of any particular one. They were "paid to think internationally," as a member of the Secretariat put it. And because they were really thinking and not merely falling into mere diplomatic discussion, we had a sense of a fresh method of approach, whether we talked to Sir Eric Drummond, to Mrs. Wicksall of the Mandates Section, or to the younger men so filled with hope for the future of the League.

Our Congress in Vienna was arranged in the midst of Austrias desolation by a group of high spirited women led by the brilliant Frau Yella Hertzka who had never during the long days of war or the ensuing peace hesitated to assert that war could achieve nothing.

And although we were so near to the great war with its millions of dead and its starved survivors, we had ventured at the very opening of the Congress to assert that war is not a natural activity for mankind, that large masses of men should fight against other large masses is abnormal, both from the biological and ethical point of view. We stated that it is a natural tendency of men to come into friendly relationships with ever larger and larger groups, and to live constantly a more extended life. It required no courage to predict that the endless desire of men would at last assert itself, that desire which torments them almost like an unappeased thirst, not to be kept apart but to come to terms with one another. It is the very spring of life which underlies all social organizations and political associations.

AN AFTER WORD

We returned to the United States in October to find the enthusiasm for the International Conference on the Limitation of Armaments, convened by President Harding for Armistice day, Nov. nth, 1921, running at full tide.

During the autumn and early winter, womens organizations of all kinds were eagerly advocating limitations of armaments and many of them had united with other public bodies in establishing headquarters in Washington from which information and propaganda were constantly issued.

Seldom had any public movement received more universal support from American women; an estimate issued by the National League of Women Voters stated that more than a million communications had been sent to Washington by individuals and organizations expressing desire for some form of an association of nations.

The Section for the United States of The Womans International League moved its headquarters from New York to Washington for the period of the Conference. Many of our National Sections in their respective capitals had held public meetings on Nov. nth advocating disarmament and those National Sections whose governments were represented at Washington had sent "manifestos" to their own Commissioners in addition to the one sent on behalf of the International body authorized at Vienna. We felt our voices but an infinitesimal strain in the chorus of praise for the Conference and while we hoped for much more than the limitation so finely advocated by Secretary Hughes we were able to unite with millions of fellow-citizens in believing the historic gathering to be an earnest of the time when friendly conference and joint responsibility shall supersede the secrecy and suspicion leading to war.

The disposition to discuss genuine world problems in a spirit of frankness and good will, in marked contrast to traditional international gatherings, led to a widespread hope that the Conference had inaugurated a precedent that might result in the successive throwing off of Committees and Commissions as required to deal with world situations and so institute a kind of world organization which should be a natural growth, in contrast although not therefore in opposition, to the carefully constituted League of Nations. It was also encouraging that the Conference exhibited an acute consciousness of the hideous state of a world facing starvation and industrial confusion. The strong public movement developed during its sessions for the immediate calling of an international conference to consider Economic problems, testified to the currency of this sense of world disaster which could no longer be confined to Europe.

Throughout these months we were all conscious of the desperate need of food for millions of the starving Russians. But whether I was serving on a committee to secure funds, lecturing before a State Agricultural Convention, asking the farmers for corn to be sent abroad in the form of meal and oil or urging congressmen to vote for an adequate appropriation with which to buy for Russia the surplus crop of grain in this country, I was constantly haunted by a sense of colossal mal-adjustment, by the lack of intelligence in international affairs. An American Quaker who came directly from the famine district in Samara told us of the desperate people living on powdered grass and roots cooked with the hoofs of horses that it might stick together in the semblance of a flat cake: that they knew full well that even such food would be exhausted by the first of the year and that unless help came from abroad, few of them could survive until spring. She told of the farm machinery left on the roadside by desperate peasants who could drag it with them no farther in their dreary search for food, of the possible abandonment of a large acreage which had for years supplied millions of people with bread. It was as if in the midst of the present starvation, dragons teeth of future misery were being sown. In December, 1921, we hailed with relief and gratitude the appropriation made by the United States Congress toward the feeding of Russia. This appropriation of twenty million dollars not only maintained the humanitarian traditions of the United States but because it openly recognized the relation between the surplus grain in America and the dearth in Russia, acknowledged the economic interdependence of nations and the necessity for more intelligent cooperation.

On the whole H. G. Wells doubtless registered a widespread reaction when he declared that throughout the Conference on the Limitation of Armaments, his moods had fluctuated between hope and despair. His final words in a remarkable series of articles so nearly express what I had heard in many countries, from our members during the summer, that I venture to quote them here:

"But I know that I believe so firmly in this great World at Peace that lies so close to our own, ready to come into being as our wills turn toward it, that I must needs go about this present world of disorder and dark ness like an exile doing such feeble things as I can towards the world of my desire, now hopefully, now bitterly, as the moods may happen before I die."

APPENDIX

Womens International League For Peace And Freeodm International Headquarters, 6, rue du Vieux-College, Geneva, Switzerland.

Imagine that you are in Geneva, that you have left behind you the lake, and the Jardin Anglais with its great fountain and have turned up the Rue dltalie. In front of you, then, you see an old grey wall, overhung with creepers, with the date 1777 let into its side, and a broad stone stairway leading up to a quaint old house in a charming garden. Here are the international headquarters of the League.

WHAT IS THIS LEAGUE?

It is a federation of women with organized sections in 21 of the most important countries, and scattered members and correspondents from Iceland to Fiji; women pledged to do everything in their power to create international relations based on good-will, making war impossible; women who seek to establish equality between men and women, and who feel the necessity of educating the coming generations to help to realize these principles.

The League is made up of people who believe that we are not obliged to choose between violence and passive acceptance of unjust conditions for ourselves or others; who believe, on the contrary, that courage, determination, moral power, generous indignation, active good-will, can achieve their ends without violence. We believe that experience condemns force as a self defeating weapon although men are still so disposed to turn to it in education, in dealing with crime, in effecting or preventing social changes, and above all in carrying out national policies. We believe that new methods, free from violence, must be worked out for ending abuses and for undoing wrongs, as well as for achieving positive ends.

CONGRESS AND SUMMER SCHOOLS

What keeps the League together is its common program as voted at its Congresses. The first of these was held at the Hague in 1915, the second at Zurich in 1919, the last at Vienna in 1921. A very successful international Summer School was held at Salzburg in August, 1921.

National Sections. The addresses of our Sections–organized national branches or correspondents–are as follows:

Austria: Frau Yella Hertzka, Hofburg,
Michaelertor, Wien I.

Australia: Miss Eleanor M. Moore, 40 Eve lina Rd., Toorak, Melbourne.
Mrs. H. S. Bayley, "Runny-
mede," Newton near Hobart,
Tasmania.

Mrs. E. A. Guy, Rockhampton,
Queensland.

Bulgaria: Mme. Anna Theodorova, Obo- richte 26, Sofia.
Mme. Jenny Dojilowa Patteff,
Bourgas.

Canada: Mrs. Harriet Dunlop Prenter, 92
Westminster Avenue, Toronto.

Denmark: Miss Thora Daugaard, Danske Kvinders Fredsbureau, Kompag-nistraede 2, Copenhagen.

Finland: Miss Annie Furuhjelm, 14 Ka- sarngaten, Helsingfors.

France: Mme. Gabrielle Duchene, 10 Ave.
de Tokio, Paris.

Germany: Frl. Lida Gustava Heymann, 12
Kaulbachstr, Miinchen.

Gr. Britain: Mrs. H. M. Swanwick, 55 Gower St., London W. C. 1.

Greece: Mme. Olga Bellini, c/o Mme.
Parren, 44 rue Epire, Athene.

Hungary: Miss Vilma Gliicklich, 41 Katona
Joszef ut., Budapest V.

Ireland: Miss Louie Bennett, 39 Harcourt
St., Dublin.

Italy: Signora Rosa Genoni, 6 Via Kra mer, Milan.

Netherlands:

New Zealand:

Norway:

Poland:

Sweden:
Switzerland:
Ukraine:
U. S. A.:
  Belgium:
Czecho-Slov.:
  Japan:
  Mexico:
Mme. Cor. Ramondt-Hirsch-
mann, 5 Valeriusplein, Amster-
dam.
Mrs. E. Gibson, 56 St. Marys
Rd., Auckland.
Miss Martha Larsen, Spndre
Huseby, Skoien, pr. Kristiania.
Mme. Daszynska-Golinska,
Wspelna79/7, Warsaw.
Miss Matilde Widegren, Sibyl-
legatan 59, Stockholm.
Mme. Clara Ragaz, 68 Gloriastr,
Zurich.
  Mile. Dr. N. Surowzowa, Chi-
manistr, 29/4, Wien XIX.
Mrs. George Odell, 1623 H St.,
Washington, D. C.
Addresses of correspondents and
corresponding societies.
Mile. Lucie Dejardin, 48 rue St.
Julienne, Liege.
  Mme. Kovarova-Machova, Pado-
kalska 1973, Prague II.
Mme. Pavla Moudra, Neveklov.
Mr. Isamu Kawakami, Corres-
pondence and Publicity Bureau,
10 Omote Sarugaku Cho Kanda,
Tokyo.
  Miss Tano Jodai, Jap. Womens
University Kaishikawa, Tokyo.
Mrs. George D. Shadbourne, Jr.,
La Mishad Apartment, 1875
Sacramento St., Sari Francisco,
Cal.
  Miss Elena Landazuri, 3a Cordoba 77, Mexico City.
  Peru: Miss Dora Mayer, Loreto altos 45, Callao.
  Roumania: Mme. Emilian, 59 rue Doro-bantzilor, Bukarest.

Jugo-Slavia: Mme. Dedier, Ministere de Po-
litique Sociale, Belgrade.
Dr. Zdenka Smrekar, Kumicic ut,
III., Zagreb.
Mme. Aloysia Stebi, Dunajska
Cesta 25, Ljubljana.
DATE DUE
DEMCO, INC. 38-2931
DATE DUE
DEMCO, INC. 38-2931

CPSIA information can be obtained at www.ICGtesting.com
Printed in the USA
LVOW100032021211

257389LV00002B/230/P

9 780217 937245